A B C OF GOTHIC ARCHITECTURE

A B C OF GOTHIC ARCHITECTURE

JOHN HENRY PARKER

ISBN: 978-93-89539-11-0

Published: 1881

LECTOR HOUSE LLP
E-MAIL: lectorpublishing@gmail.com

A B C OF GOTHIC ARCHITECTURE,

BY

JOHN HENRY PARKER, C.B.

Hon. M.A. Oxon, F.S.A. Lond.;
Keeper of the Ashmolean Museum, Oxford;

VICE-PRESIDENT OF THE OXFORD ARCHITECTURAL AND HISTORICAL
SOCIETY, AND OF THE BRITISH AND AMERICAN ARCHÆOLOGICAL
SOCIETY OF ROME; MEMBRE DE LA SOCIÉTÉ FRANÇAISE
D'ARCHÉOLOGIE; HONORARY MEMBER OF THE ROYAL
INSTITUTE OF BRITISH ARCHITECTS, ETC.

1881.

ADVERTISEMENT TO FIRST EDITION.

THIS little work is intended to serve as a stepping-stone to larger and more expensive works on the same subject, such as my "Introduction to the Study of Gothic Architecture," my edition of Rickman's "Gothic Architecture," and the "Glossary of Architecture." The same examples are not used, except a few well-known historical instances. My object has been to make it as simple and as easy as possible, so that a child may understand it. Experience shews that a child who has seen many examples, and has had the peculiar features of each style explained, does understand and remember them in a manner that appears astonishing to older people, and accurate representations of buildings of each period may be equally well understood and remembered. The knowledge thus acquired, simple and easy as it seems, and as it really is, if proper attention is given to it, will be found useful in after life, not in all parts of England only, but in all parts of Europe also. The general characteristic features of each period are the same, although the provincial character sometimes seems to preponderate; the character of *each century*, at all events, is the same all over Europe, and may also be easily remembered, and as a matter of fact is never forgotten.

JOHN HENRY PARKER, C.B.

OXFORD,
July, 1881.

CONTENTS

A. B. C. OF GOTHIC ARCHITECTURE.

INTRODUCTION.

ARCHITECTURAL History can only be understood by the eye, either by seeing the buildings themselves, with time to examine the construction and the details of each period, or by accurate representations of them arranged in chronological order. This is what has been attempted in the present work; and when so arranged, any one, however ignorant of the subject, can see and understand the gradual progress and change from one generation to another. What is thus understood is also easily remembered; we can always remember what we have seen, much better than what we have only heard or read about; an accurate representation of each object is better than many pages of description, or of essays about it. The arrangement made in this little work will enable any one to understand the general principles of what are called the styles or periods of Gothic Architecture. Some persons object to this name, which was undoubtedly given originally in contempt by the admirers of the Palladian style, but it has been so generally adopted all over Europe for the last century or more, that it would be in vain to attempt to change it; it is a convenient name, which everybody understands as a general term for the different styles of MEDIÆVAL ARCHITECTURE. Dr. E. A. Freeman has ingeniously suggested that it is the architecture of the Gothic nations who conquered the Roman Empire, and one of which to be proud rather than ashamed.

Strictly speaking, the Norman is one of the Romanesque styles, which succeeded to the old Roman; but the Gothic was so completely developed from the Norman, that it is impossible to draw a line of distinction between them; it is also convenient to begin with the Norman, because the earliest complete buildings that we have in this country are of the Norman period, and the designs of the Norman architects, at the end of the eleventh century and the beginning of the twelfth, were on so grand a scale, that many of our finest cathedrals are built on the foundations of the church of that period, and a great part of the walls are frequently found to be really Norman in construction, although their appearance is so entirely altered that it is difficult at first to realize this; for instance, in the grand cathedral of Winchester, William of Wykeham did not rebuild it, but so entirely altered the appearance, that it is now properly considered as one of the earliest examples of the English Perpendicular style of which he was the inventor; this style is entirely confined to England, it is readily distinguished from any of the Continental styles by the *perpendicular lines* in the tracery of the windows, and in the panelling on the walls; in all the foreign styles these lines are flowing or flame-like, and for that reason they are called Flamboyant; a few windows with tracery of that style are met with in England, but they are quite exceptions.

Some persons who object to the name of Gothic, would use the name of Pointed instead; this name was proposed by the Cambridge Camden Society about half-a-century ago, but had never got into general use, and is now seldom met with. I always objected to it, on the ground that it misleads beginners in the study, who invariably consider every round-headed doorway as Norman, and every square-headed window as Perpendicular, which is very far from being the case. The form of the arch is always dictated by convenience, and is in itself no guide to the age or style of a building; the only safe guides are the moldings and details, and these require some study, but are not at all difficult to understand or remember, when a good series of examples are put before us, as I hope will be found by those who use this little book.

I should mention that this is not at all intended to supersede my "Introduction to the Study of Gothic Architecture," but rather to serve as a stepping-stone to it, just as that leads people to want my edition of Rickman's work, with the historical additions that I have made to it.

Rickman was the first to reduce chaos into order, and to shew that the age of a building can be ascertained by the construction and the details, on the principle of comparison with well-known dated examples, and he should always have the credit of being the first to establish this. His work was at first thought rather hard reading, and this was natural, because he trusted too much to words only; my "Glossary of Architecture" was called "Rickman made easy," and this is true, because, by means of the excellent and accurate woodcuts of Orlando Jewitt, I was able to explain all the technical words which Rickman was obliged to use. In the present work I have avoided the use of these as much as possible, and have trusted to the eye in the numerous examples given, rather than to any words to explain them. The same persons who objected to the name of Gothic, objected also to the name of Early English for the earliest Gothic style in England; but this was undoubtedly developed from the Norman, in England, earlier than anywhere else.

The earliest pure and complete Gothic building in the world is St. Hugh's choir at Lincoln, which was built between 1192 and 1200, St. Hugh himself having died just before the consecration in the latter year. Of this we have distinct evidence in the life of the good bishop (who was called a saint) by his domestic chaplain, the original MS. of which is preserved in the Bodleian Library, and it has only been published in my time, at my suggestion—through Sir Duffus Hardy, the assistant Keeper of the Rolls—by the Master of the Rolls in the Government series of Chronicles. The best-informed French antiquaries acknowledge that they have nothing like it in France for thirty years afterwards; they thought it was copied from Notre Dame at Dijon, to which there is considerable resemblance, but that church was not consecrated till 1230, so that the Dijon architect might have copied from the Lincoln one, but the Lincoln could not have copied from Dijon.

In England this style is only a natural development from the Norman, in which the transition had been going on for half-a-century before. At the time of the rebuilding of the choir at Canterbury, the change was making rapid progress, the work of William the Englishman there is considerably in advance of that of his teacher, William of Sens, who began the rebuilding. The eastern transepts and the Corona of Canterbury, finished in 1184, approach very near to Gothic.

The small church of Clee at the mouth of the Humber, of which the chancel and transepts and central tower were rebuilding almost at that time, are still more Gothic, and this work was consecrated by S. Hugh in 1192, as recorded by an inscription; this was the very year in which he began rebuilding the choir at Lincoln, which was finished, as we have said, in 1200. Many of the churches of the rich Norman Abbeys in the south of Yorkshire, and north of Lincolnshire, are nearly as much advanced at the same period; and the west end of the great abbey church at St. Alban's, begun by De Cella about A.D. 1200, is also pure Gothic: of this, unfortunately, we have only a few remains.

In this work I have purposely omitted the remains of Roman villas, and of the churches between the Roman and the Norman period, of which the remains are more numerous than is generally supposed, especially the substructures, or crypts as they are called, and there are several churches of the eleventh century that do not belong to the Norman style. The Saxons appear to have been more advanced in the fine arts such as Sculpture than the Normans, but their churches were on comparatively a small scale, and were generally swept away by the Normans as not worth preserving: every one of our cathedrals was rebuilt by the Normans, and not always exactly on the same site, the old church being sometimes kept for use whilst the new one was building. Although these remains are of great interest to the antiquary, they have nothing to do with the history of Gothic architecture, which is certainly developed from the Norman, and the change did not begin till after the middle of the twelfth century, or about a century after the introduction of this style by Edward the Confessor: the remains of his abbey at Westminster are clearly Norman, and quite distinct from the Saxon character, but this style is called by the French antiquaries ANGLO-NORMAN, and this is quite correct. Normandy was then a province of the dominions of the King of England, and there are scarcely any buildings in Normandy earlier than the time of the Conquest.

The best-informed Norman antiquaries at the time of the revival of the study of Architectural History, between 1830 and 1840, made a series of excursions to the sites of all the castles of the barons who came over to England with William the Conqueror, in search of some *masonry* of the first half of the eleventh century. To their surprise, they found *no masonry at all* in any one of them; there were magnificent earthworks to all of them, clearly shewing that castles of that period were of earthworks and wood only. This is recorded in the *Bulletin Monumental* of the period, and the substance of the observations is given in the *ABCédaire* of De Caumont[1], who was their leader.

It is a mistake to suppose that the Normans brought this style with them "ready cut and dried," it began in Normandy and in England simultaneously; the

[1] *Abécédaire, ou Rudiment D'Archeologie, par M. de Caumont, fondateur des Congrès Scientifiques de France, etc.* (Caen, 1850, 8vo.)

two great abbey churches at Caen were both built after the Conquest, and with English money, and they are not at all in advance of similar buildings in England; both had originally wooden roofs and ceilings only, the stone vaults were not put on until a century after they were built; we have no stone vaults over a space of 20 ft. wide before the middle of the twelfth century, either in England or Normandy. It seemed necessary to say a few words about Normandy, but for any further information about architecture in France or in other parts of Europe, I must refer the reader to my "Introduction," in which I have given a good deal of information on the subject from personal observation.

In the present work I have purposely made long extracts from my "Introduction," on the general character of each style, which are very often the words of Rickman himself, because I could only have said the same thing in other words, and this would rather confuse students than assist them. I have selected other examples, so that one should not be a repetition of the other in the material point, the teaching by the eye; and in those examples where I saw that a few words of description would be useful, they are added, so that this work is complete in itself for beginners, but those who wish to go on further with the subject can do so step by step. The only real way of thoroughly understanding Architectural History, is to go about and see the buildings themselves.

THE EARLY NORMAN PERIOD.A.D. 1060-1090.

THE Norman style was introduced into England in the time of Edward the Confessor; the king himself founded the great Abbey of Westminster, and many of the buildings were begun in his time. Of this church he had completed the choir and transepts, which were sufficient for the performance of divine service, and it was then consecrated, Dec. 28, 1065, a few days only before his death. As soon as the choir of a church was ready for Divine Service, it was usual to consecrate it: the nave was called the vestibule, and was not consecrated. The nave of Westminster at that time was not built: it is probable that a nave was built in the twelfth century, but of this church we have no remains. The dormitory was in all probability building at the same time, as the monks or canons who had to perform the service in the church must have required a place to sleep in. Of this dormitory the walls and the vaulted substructure remain. The refectory also was begun at the same period, and we have the lower part of the walls, with the arcade

Westminster Abbey, A.D. 1066.

The Dark Cloister under the Dormitory, now the Schoolroom, and Windows of
the Dormitory.

at the foot; the work is rude and clumsy Norman, with wide-jointed masonry,
and the capitals left plain, to be painted or carved afterwards.

Soon after the Norman Conquest a great change took place in the art of building in England. On consulting the history of our cathedral churches, we find that

in almost every instance the church was rebuilt from its foundations by the first Norman bishop, either on the same site or on a new one; sometimes, as at Norwich and Peterborough, the cathedral was removed to a new town altogether, and built on a spot where there was no church before; in other cases, as at Winchester, the new church was built near the old one, which was not pulled down until after the relics had been translated with great pomp from the old church to the new. In other instances, as at York and Canterbury, the new church was erected on the site of the old one, which was pulled down piecemeal as the new work progressed. These new churches were in all cases on a much larger and more magnificent scale than the old; they were also constructed in a much better manner, the Normans being far better masons than the Saxons[2].

Doorway, Dartford, Gundulph, A.D. 1080.   Westminster Abbey, A.D. 1066.

---

[2] There is some doubt on this subject; the opinion here stated is that generally received, but recent observations seem to shew that the Saxons were more advanced than the Normans at the time of the Conquest; their work was more highly finished, had more ornament, and they used fine-jointed masonry, while the Normans used wide-jointed, but the Norman buildings were more substantial, and on a larger scale; everywhere the cathedrals were rebuilt after the Conquest.

Rubble Masonry, from Gundulph's Tower, called St. Leonard's, at Malling, Kent, A.D. 1070.

The earliest Norman Keep in existence.

Notwithstanding this superiority of workmanship to that which had preceded it, the *early* Norman masonry is extremely rude and bad; the joints between the stones are often from one inch to two or three inches wide, and filled with mortar not always of very good quality. In consequence of this imperfect construction, many of the towers fell down within a few years after their erection. It is probable, however, that the workmen employed on these structures were for the most part Saxons, as the Normans must have been too much employed otherwise during the reign of the Conqueror to execute much masons' work with their own hands. Nor were the Norman monks established in sufficient numbers to be able to superintend all the

Westminster Abbey, A.D. 1066.

Arcade of the Refectory, now in a Canon's garden.

works which were going on at this period; the cathedrals and large monasteries must have occupied nearly all their attention. The ordinary parish churches which required rebuilding must have been left to the Saxons themselves, and were probably built in the same manner as before, with such slight improvements as they might have gleaned from the Norman works.

The Normans themselves were, however, but little in advance of the English in the building art: the style which we call Norman correctly for this country, is called by the French archæologists ANGLO-NORMAN, and with reason; that style was developed as much in England as in Normandy.

GUNDULPH, Bishop of Rochester, was the great architect of the time of William the Conqueror. The first building of his that we have remaining is the keep of his castle at Malling, in Kent, called St. Leonard's Tower, which was built about 1070. This is of earlier character than any keep in Normandy. M. de Caumont examined the sites of the castles of all the barons who came over to England with William, and he found no masonry of that period in any one of them. Their castles had consisted of very fine earthworks and wood only[3]. Soon after this time,

Early Norman Keep at Malling, Kent, built by Gundulph A.D, 1070.

Gundulph built the keep of the castle in London called the White Tower, and the cathedral of Rochester, of which we have a part of the crypt, and some remains of the wall of the nave and north transept. The whole of this work is extremely rude; the construction is usually rubble. When of ashlar, the joints are very wide, and the capitals of the shafts clumsy.

---

[3] This is recorded in the *Bulletin Monumental* of the period, and in the *Abécédaire* of M. de Caumont.

Wide-jointed Masonry, Chapel in the White Tower, London, A.D. 1081.

St. Alban's Abbey Church, built in the time of William the Conqueror and William Rufus, as distinctly recorded by contemporary historians, partakes of the Saxon character in many parts: we find baluster shafts in abundance, quantities of Roman tiles, and other features usually considered Saxon, but there is not the slightest doubt that the church was built from the foundations after 1077, when the work was commenced by Abbot Paul of Caen. The materials of an older church are used in it; they were probably brought from old Verulam, with the Roman flat bricks, which are largely used in the construction.

We have a strong confirmation of this in the city of Lincoln: the Conqueror having taken possession of about a quarter of the old city to build a castle upon, and Bishop Remigius having purchased nearly another quarter to build a cathedral and monastery, the Saxon inhabitants were driven down the hill on which the old city stands, and took possession of some swampy land at the foot of the hill, which they drained, and redeemed from the fens or marshes of which nearly all the low country then consisted. On this new land they built several churches. One of these, St. Peter's at Gowts (or at the Sluices), remains nearly entire, and St. Mary le Wig-ford has retained the tower built at this period. This is an important and interesting fact in the history of architecture, as it confirms what was before only a natural supposition, and it enables us to fill up a gap: we appeared to have scarcely any parish churches of the early Norman period, but it is now evident that many of the long list of churches of the Anglo-Saxon type belong to a period subsequent to the Conquest. The tower of St. Michael's Church, Oxford, is one of those included by Rickman as of the character supposed to be Saxon, but the imposts of the window-arches are quite of Norman character, and it was built after the Conquest. The tower of Oxford Castle was built by Robert D'Oyly in the time of William Rufus, but it has much of the appearance of the Saxon buildings, and the tower of St. Michael's Church is part of the work of his time. Round towers built of rubble-stone are of several periods, generally early, but in a mere rubble wall there is nothing to go by as to the date; they may be of any period.

It is customary to date the introduction of the Norman style into England from the Norman Conquest, in 1066, although that important event had no *immediate* effect on the style of Architecture, and perhaps the remainder of the eleventh century may be considered as a period of transition, just as the last quarter of each of the three following centuries was a period of transition from one style to another; and it may be well to observe, that in all such periods, not only were buildings of a mixed character erected, but some buildings were almost entirely in the old style, others altogether in the new one: this has been called by Professor Willis "an overlapping of the styles," and generally lasts from twenty to thirty years. In treating of the Norman period we must bear in mind that Normandy was then a province of the same kingdom, and that the intercourse between Kent and Normandy was at least as frequent and as easy as between Yorkshire and Devonshire; so that although there are certain marked provincialisms, there is no real difference or priority of style in one province over the other, after the Norman power was fully established in England. It is customary to point to the two great abbey churches at Caen, founded and endowed by William and Matilda, as models to be referred to, and as proving the great advance of Normandy over England; but this is, in a great degree, a mistake, arising from the common error of confusing the date of the foundation of a monastery with that of the erection of the existing church: a small part only of the church of St. Stephen at Caen is of the time of the Conqueror, and a still smaller part of that of the Holy Trinity, the present building of which is considerably later than the other. In both of these fine churches, the vaults, and the upper parts of the structure, were built late in the twelfth century; they had originally wooden roofs only.

The most important buildings of the time of the Conqueror and of William Rufus were the Norman castles or keep-towers, but most of these were rebuilt in the following century. The earliest Norman keep existing is the one built immediately after the Conquest, by Gundulph, at Malling in Kent, miscalled St. Leonard's tower, as already mentioned [see page 17]. There are still some Norman keeps of this period remaining, as London; but Dover and Rochester in Kent, Newcastle in Northumberland, Appleby and Carlisle in Cumberland, Brougham in Westmoreland, Richmond and Conisborough in Yorkshire, Porchester in Hampshire, Guildford in Surrey, Goodrich in Herefordshire, Norwich and Castle Rising in Norfolk, Hedingham and Colchester in Essex, are later, and belong chiefly to the twelfth century; but most of them, if not all, were *founded* at this early period. Rochester has been entirely rebuilt on another site. From the uniformity of plan—a massive square tower, with a square turret at each angle of small projection, and a flat buttress up the centre of each face—and the general plainness of the work, it requires a careful examination of each of these buildings to ascertain to which period it belongs. The only parts where any ornament is to be found are usually the entrance-doorway and staircase, and the chapel, and these are commonly rather late

Norman. There is frequently a solid wall in the middle, dividing the keep into two portions, with no communication in the lower parts. The passages for communication between one part of the building and another are made in the thickness of the wall, the central part having been divided by floors only, and not vaulted, in the earlier examples. Groined stone vaults, of rough stone, were introduced towards the end of the eleventh century in castles as well as churches; but rib-vaulting of cut stone not before the twelfth.

The number of churches which were commenced in the reign of the Conqueror and his successor was so great, that it is impossible to notice them all: but few of them were completed until after 1100; it was not, indeed, until after 1080 that the country was sufficiently settled for much building to be begun.

The chapel in the White Tower, London, is one of the best and most perfect examples of this period; its character is massive and plain, though the work is well executed. Its plan is oblong, consisting of a nave with narrow aisles which stand on the thickness of the walls: the walls have passages in them also in the other parts; the nave has plain barrel-vaults; the pillars are short and thick, and most of the capitals are plain, but some have a little ornament carved upon the abacus and capital, apparently some time after the construction was completed, being within easy reach.

The nave and transepts of Ely were erected by Abbot Simeon, brother of Bishop Walkelyn. Part of the west front of Lincoln was built by Bishop Remi, or Remigius, 1085-1092: the small portion which remains of this work is a very valuable specimen of early Norman, the more so that the insertion of later and richer Norman doorways by Bishop Alexander, about fifty years afterwards, enables us to compare early and late Norman work, while the jointing of the masonry leaves no doubt of the fact that these doorways are insertions, and therefore confirms the early date of the three lofty arches under which they are inserted. A comparison of the capitals and details of these two periods, thus placed in juxtaposition, is extremely interesting. The wide-jointing of the masonry and the shallowness of the carving distinguish the old work from the new. Several capitals of the later period are inserted in the older work, as is shewn on careful examination by the jointing of the masonry, and by the form of the capitals themselves: the earlier capitals are short, and have volutes at the angles, forming a sort of rude Ionic; the later capitals are more elongated, and have a sort of rude Corinthian, or Composite foliage.

The crypt and transepts of Winchester Cathedral are of this period, built by Bishop Walkelyn on a new site. Early in the twelfth century occurred the fall of the tower of this Cathedral, celebrated from the peculiar circumstances with which it was accompanied, which are thus described by William of Malmesbury, who was living at the time:—"A few countrymen conveyed the body [of the king, William Rufus], placed

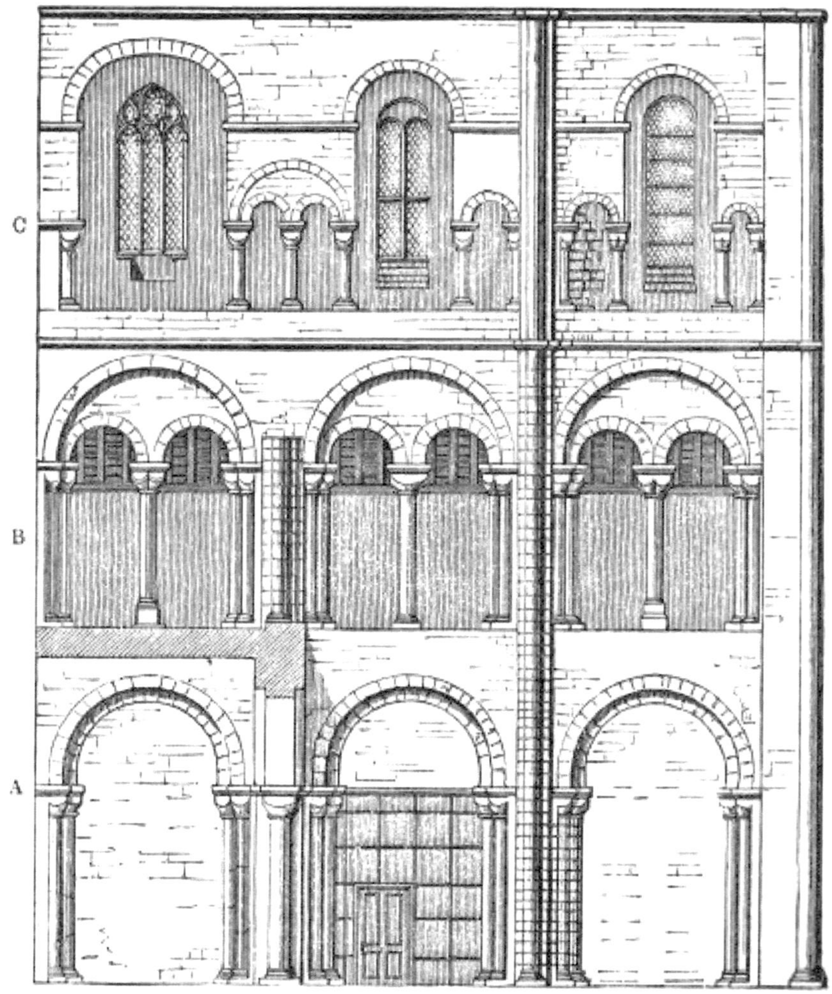

Transept, Winchester Cathedral, A.D. 1079-1093.

A. Pier-arches.

B. Triforium, or Blind-story.

C. Clear-story, or Clere-story.

N.B. It may be noted that the pier-arches, triforium, and clerestory, are all nearly of equal height, which is frequent in Roman basilicas and in the Norman style, but not afterwards.

on a cart, to the cathedral of Winchester, the blood dripping from it all the way. Here it was committed to the ground *within the tower*, attended by many of the nobility, but lamented by few. The next year (1097) the tower fell; though I forbear to mention the different opinions on this subject, lest I should seem to assent too readily to unsupported trifles; more especially that the building might have fallen *through imperfect construction*, even though he had never been buried there."

That this was really the case, the building itself affords us abundant evidence, and proves that even the Normans at this period were still bad masons, and very imperfectly acquainted with the principles of construction. The tower which was rebuilt soon after the fall is still standing, and the enormous masses of masonry which were piled together to support it, and prevent it from falling again, shew such an amazing waste of labour and material as clearly to prove that it was the work of very unskilful builders.

This example is valuable to us also in another respect: the two transepts were only partially injured by the fall of the tower; the greater part of both of them belongs to the original work; the junction of the old work and the new can be distinctly traced; and here we begin to find a difference of character in the new work, and a mark by which we can

Bay, Winchester Cathedral, c. A.D. 1095.

The window is an insertion of the fourteenth century in the Decorated style.

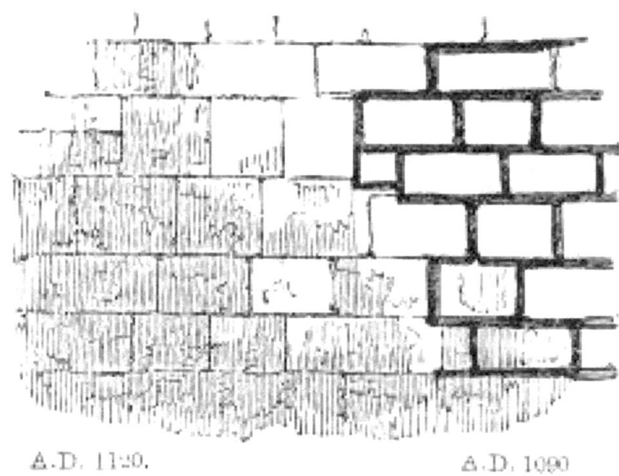

A.D. 1120. A.D. 1090.

Winchester Cathedral, Transept.

readily distinguish one from the other: the joints between the stones in the old work are wide, filled with a great thickness of mortar; in the new work they are comparatively fine, often leaving room for scarcely more than to pass a knife: the one is called "wide-jointed masonry," the other "fine-jointed masonry," and this is the best and safest distinction between early and late Norman work; the rule is almost of universal application. In confirmation of this we may cite another passage from William of Malmesbury, describing the work of his own time, and what he had probably seen himself:— "He [Roger, Bishop of Salisbury] was a prelate of great mind, and spared no expense towards completing his designs, especially in buildings; which may be seen in other places, but more particularly at Salisbury and at Malmesbury, for there he erected extensive edifices at vast cost, and with surpassing beauty, *the courses of stone being so correctly laid that the joint deceives the eye,*

St. John's Church, Chester.   **Winchester Cathedral, A.D. 1079-1093.**

One Bay of Choir, c. A.D. 1075-1095.

and leads it to imagine that the whole wall is composed of a single block." The buildings here alluded to were erected between 1115 and 1139, this may then fairly be considered as the turning-point between early and late Norman work; and here it will be convenient to pause in our history, and describe the characteristic features of early Norman work.

St. John's Church at Chester, which was the seat of the Bishop, or cathedral, until the time of Henry VIII., was built A.D. 1075-1095, and is one of the finest examples of the Early Norman style. (See 29.)

No clear line of distinction can be drawn between the three periods into which the Norman style is naturally divided. They run into each other, and overlap each other continually; there is no broad line between them: yet there is a very marked difference between the early Norman of the original parts of Westminster Abbey, shewn at pp. 11 and 13, of the time of Edward the Confessor, and the rich doorways and windows of Iffley, Cuddesdon, and Middleton Stoney, shewn at pp. 45 and 49, which are of the time of Henry II., or rather more than a century after those of Westminster Abbey.

THE NORMAN PERIOD, A.D. 1090-1150.

We have now arrived at the period of those RICH NORMAN CHURCHES which may still be considered as amongst the glories of our land.

It is very remarkable that so large a number of buildings of the rich character which generally distinguishes this style should all have been built in about half a century, from 1120 to 1170 or 1180; yet such is clearly the case. The early Norman style has been already described; the late or rich Norman is chiefly characterized by the abundance of ornament and the deep cutting, the absence of which is the chief characteristic of the earlier period.

Before we proceed to describe it, a few of the buildings known to have been erected at this time may be mentioned.

Peterborough Cathedral was begun from its foundations in 1117 by John de Seez, who formed the plan of the whole of it, which was rigidly carried out by his successors, and it was consecrated in 1143; the work is very good, but not very rich. The Norman tower at Bury St. Edmund's was commenced in the same year, 1117, and finished in 1130; the porch is an addition about half a century later. The nave of Norwich was built between 1122 and 1145: the work is still very plain, being in continuation of the previous work. Castor Church, Northamptonshire, bears an inscription recording its dedication in 1124: the tower is good, rich Norman work; the ornaments are the hatched, the square billet, and the scollop, all of very simple character, shallow, and easily worked. Furness Abbey was founded in 1127, but very little of the original work remains. In Canterbury Cathedral, the work of Prior Ernulf, under St. Anselm, was completed in 1130, and part of Rochester, where Ernulf had become bishop, in the same year; so that we need not be surprised at finding more ornament in these two cathedrals than is quite consistent with the usual character of early Norman work, and the same ornaments repeated in both these churches. St. Martin's priory at Dover was founded in 1131; the refectory is still standing, and is a good example of plain Norman work, neither very early nor very late.

The small Norman church of Newhaven in Sussex is unusually perfect, and gives a good general idea of a parish church of the twelfth century. At first sight it looks earlier than it is; the bold projection of the buttresses indicates a later period, early Norman buttresses are very flat, the greater the projection the later

Newhaven Church, Sussex, c. A.D. 1120.

The apse is usually an early feature; in this instance the projection of the buttresses and the ornamental string round it shew it to be later. The side-window is an insertion in the Early English style.

they are, as a general rule. The spire is an early one, though that is not likely to be Norman. The belfry-windows in the tower, and the corbel-table under the eaves of the roof, are early. The porch is evidently a later addition.

At Iffley the tower is later; the original choir was square, with a flat east end, and another square bay has been added eastward at a later period, more in the Early English style.

The Augustinian priory of Dunstable, in Bedfordshire, was also founded in 1131; the original parts of the west front and of the nave are remarkably fine and rich Norman work.

In the time of William Rufus the work begun by the Norman bishops was carried on so vigorously, that, before the close of this century, *every one* of the Saxon cathedrals was undergoing the same process of destruction, to be rebuilt on a larger scale and in a better manner. Some of the buildings which remain to us of the work of this reign are the crypt of Worcester; the crypt, the arches of the nave, and part of the transepts of Gloucester; the choir and transepts of Durham; the nave and transepts of Christchurch in Hampshire; the choir and transepts of Norwich.

The history of Canterbury Cathedral has been so carefully preserved by contemporary records, and these have been so thoroughly investigated by Professor Willis, and compared with the existing structure, that we may almost put a date upon every stone of this magnificent fabric; it is therefore our best and safest guide in the study of the architecture of that period in England. The work in the older part of the crypt agrees exactly with that at Lincoln, and the other early Norman works above mentioned. The crypt is, however, not part of Lanfranc's work, for it is remarkable that his church was entirely pulled down and rebuilt by his successor, St. Anselm, between 1096 and 1110, under the direction of Priors Ernulf and Conrad. Even in the time of Gervase, writing in 1170, he says, "You must know, however, good reader, that I never saw the choir of Lanfranc, neither have I been able to meet with any description of it: Eadmer indeed describes the old church, which before the time of Lanfranc was constructed after the Roman manner; he also mentions, but does not describe, the work of Lanfranc, which succeeded this old church, and the choir of Conrad, constructed in the time of St. Anselm." From this we may fairly conclude that the work of Lanfranc was of very inferior character. It is now said by some, that parts of the walls of the present crypt at the west end belong to this early period, "after the Roman manner;" Willis considered this to be of the time of Lanfranc.

During the first fifteen or twenty years of the twelfth century, and of the reign of Henry I., there was no perceptible change of style; the numerous great works which had been begun during the preceding twenty years were carried on, and many of them were completed. During this period we have the dedications, — which shew that the work was sufficiently forward *for the choir* to be used, — of Ely, Rochester, Norwich, Canterbury, and some others. Several new works were commenced also, as Tewkesbury Abbey, St. Botolph's, Colchester, St. Bartholomew's, Smithfield, the nave of Durham, the choir of Peterborough, and Reading Abbey: but we do not find any difference between the early parts of these and those which immediately preceded them. There is no difference whatever between those built on the sites of the Saxon cathedrals, and those which were now first erected on entirely new sites.

We find in early Norman work that the chisel was very little used; most of the ornaments are such as could be readily worked with the axe, and whatever sculpture there is appears to have been executed afterwards, for it was a general practice to execute sculpture after the stones were placed, as is evident in the early work at Westminster: some of the capitals in the crypt of Canterbury are only half finished to this day, the work of carving having probably gone on until it was stopped by the great fire in 1174. If the sculpture is early it is very rude, and the work is shallow. But shallowness of carving depends partly on the nature of the material to be carved; from this cause buildings of a hard stone, such as granite, often appear much older than they really are. Baptismal fonts especially are frequently made of hard stone or marble, which admit of shallow sculpture; and rich Norman work cut shallow may be found as late as the time of Henry II.

Crypt, Canterbury, A.D. 1110.

Norman capital, with carving commenced and left unfinished.

Although the roofs of the aisles at Canterbury had been vaulted, the choir itself had a flat boarded ceiling, painted like that still remaining at Peterborough. The vault of the choir of the cathedral of Sens, from whence came William, the architect of the choir of Canterbury, is also an addition of later date. The same change was made in many other churches of that period. The builders of the early Norman period did not venture to erect a vault over so large a space; we do not find any early vault over a space above twenty feet wide, and few of so wide a span. Many of our Norman cathedrals still have timber roofs over the large spaces, and the aisles vaulted. In Normandy vaults were more frequently used than in England, even at this early period; and this was still more the case in subsequent times, for the fine open timber roofs for which some parts of England are distinguished are unknown in Normandy, where almost every village church is vaulted over.

Here it may be well to mention, that down to the early Norman period the eastern limb of a cruciform church, or the chancel of a plain oblong plan, was always short, rarely more than a single square, or at the utmost two squares, in length, and was frequently terminated by a round east end called an apse. Immediately after this period the custom of lengthening the eastern limb of the church became so general, that the original dimensions have been almost lost sight of. The history of nearly every one of our cathedrals gives the same result: first, the choir was lengthened by the addition of a presbytery, and afterwards still further by adding a lady-chapel, which did not come into fashion until quite the end of the twelfth century.

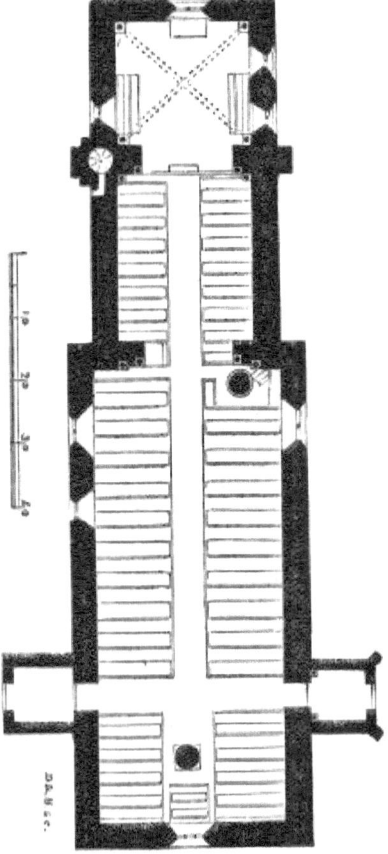

Ground-plan of Cassington Church.

Gervase and William of Malmesbury have furnished us, as we have seen, with a clue by which to distinguish the work of the early Norman period from that of a later age, namely, wide-jointed masonry, and shallow sculpture executed chiefly with the axe instead of the chisel. The best and safest test is the wide-jointed masonry, where it is found; but in some cases the joints can hardly be said to be either wide or fine; they are of a moderate width, and not of marked character either way.

The *arch* is generally at first not recessed at all, afterwards only once recessed, and the edges are either square, or have a plain round molding cut upon them; the zigzag *ornament* is used, but not so abundantly as at a later period; the dripstone is frequently ornamented with what is called the hatched molding; the billet is also used, but sparingly, and perhaps not before 1100; it is found in the early parts of Peterborough, but not in the later parts. The head of the door is generally square with a round arch over it, and the intermediate space under the arch, called the tympanum, is either left plain, or ornamented with shallow sculpture of rude character, sometimes preserved from an earlier building.

Rich Doorways form one of the most important features of late Norman work. The examples given from Cuddesdon and Middleton Stoney are good ordinary specimens, such as may be found in scores of parish churches. They are generally round-headed, very deeply recessed, and frequently have shafts in the jambs. The tympanum is frequently filled with rich sculpture, which becomes deeper and better executed as the style advances. The moldings are numerous, but not of much variety in section,

NORMAN DOORWAYS.

Cuddesdon, Oxon, c. A.D. 1160.   Middleton Stoney, Oxon, c. A.D. 1160.

consisting chiefly of round and quarter-round members, but all preserving a general square outline. These moldings, however, as well as the jambs and shafts, are frequently entirely overlaid with ornament, which, though of a peculiar and somewhat rude character, produces great richness of effect; and few features of churches are more generally admired than these rich Norman doorways, which are very abundant in many parts of the country, quite as much so as in Normandy itself. The examples in England are quite as fine and as numerous in proportion as in Normandy; and these doorways were so much admired for their rich character, that they have often been preserved when the church has been rebuilt, perhaps several times. The doorways of Iffley Church are among the richest that we have anywhere; not only the very fine one at the west end, but the north and south doors.

NORMAN WINDOWS are in general long and rather narrow round-headed openings, but sometimes of two lights divided by a shaft, included under one arch, more especially in belfries; in rich buildings they are frequently ornamented in the same manner as the doorways, with recessed arches, zig-zag and other moldings, as at Iffley, Oxfordshire, and sometimes with sculpture; other examples have shafts in the jambs carrying the

NORMAN WINDOWS.

**Belfry Window, Northleigh, Oxon, c.   Bucknell, Oxon, c. A.D. 1150.
A.D. 1100.**

Window, Exterior.   **Interior, Handborough, Oxon, c. A.D. 1120.**

arch-moldings, and others are quite plain. At Castle Rising, Norfolk, is a very rich late example, with intersecting arcades on each side, ornamented chiefly with the lozenge molding. In Romsey Abbey, Hampshire, Waltham Abbey, Essex, Christ Church Cathedral, Oxford, and very many other examples, the clerestory window has a smaller blind arch on each side of it, making a triple opening within to a single window; and the shafts of this triple opening are made to carry small shafts to the upper arches. This is a common arrangement of Norman clerestory windows: at St. Stephen's, Caen, there is only one subarch to each light instead of two, but this arises from the arrangement of the sexpartite vaulting.

St. John, Devizes, c. A.D. 1160.

The fine circular windows with wheel-like divisions belong to this period: Barfreston, in Kent, is a good example. St. James, Bristol, is a singular one, the effect of which is rich and good. There was frequently one in the centre of the west front, which was called the oculus, or eye of the building. These large round windows are much more common on the Continent than in England. In Italy there are many fine examples, as at Toscanella, Perugia, and Assisi. The French also appear to have always had a particular fondness for this kind of window, which in the later styles becomes the magnificent rose-window, so often the glory of the French churches.

St. James, Bristol.

Norman windows are far less common than the doorways, having frequently been destroyed to make room for those of later styles; probably for the purpose of introducing the painted glass of those periods, which did not suit well with the early windows. Small circular openings are also a common feature, as in the clerestory of Southwell Minster. The zigzag molding is frequently used in the arches of windows, as at St. John's, Devizes, p. 44; occasionally, but not so frequently, this ornament is also carried down the jambs, as at Iffley. Windows of two lights divided by a mullion were not introduced until after the Norman period. The walls being generally very thick, the opening is small and narrow on the outside of the wall, and is very widely splayed to admit more light; so that while the glass is less than a foot wide, the opening of the splay on the inner side of the wall is three feet wide.

Iffley, Oxon, c. A.D. 1166.

THE ARCHES are generally round-headed: in early work they are plain and square-edged, with or without a recess at the angle; sometimes doubly recessed, and still square-edged, as in the early work at Westminster, p. 11, the White Tower, London, and the transept of Winchester, p. 27; sometimes molded, with plain round moldings. In the later period they are more richly molded than in the early part of the style: the chancel-arch especially is very much enriched; and the western side, facing the spectator when looking towards the altar, is generally much more ornamented than the eastern side. The chancel-arch at Iffley is one of the richest and best examples: where there is a central tower, as in that instance, both the tower-arches across the church are usually ornamented in the same manner; the side-arches, where there are transepts, are frequently much plainer, and often pointed. In the later part of the Norman style, without any other change, they are still quite plain and square-edged. In this manner the pointed arch occurs quite as early as 1150, or even earlier; at a later period they become much more common, and are gradually developed into the Early English style, which some call the "first pointed style;" but the pointed arch alone does not make a change of style.

THE SMALL ARCADES which are frequently used as decorations of the walls, and for sedilia, have scarcely any separate character; they are diminutives of the larger arches, except that the shafts are smaller and shorter in proportion: in rich work they are used both inside and outside of the walls, and frequently on the outside of the clerestory, as well as on the inside in front of the blind-story, now called the triforium. Intersecting arches occur in these arcades from a very early period; and Rickman observes, that whoever constructed them, constructed pointed arches; and he adds, "It appears as if the round and pointed arches were for nearly a century used indiscriminately, as was most consonant to the necessities of the work, or the builder's ideas." At Canterbury, an ornamental arcade of intersecting arches occurs both on the inside and outside of the wall in St. Anselm's tower.

In the apse in the White Tower the arches are stilted to accommodate them to their position. The arches of the triforium are generally wide and low; sometimes they are divided by two sub-arches.

The form of the arch was at all periods dictated partly by convenience, and is not to be relied on as a guide to the date or style; but there was a prevailing fashion, and that form was usually followed at each period, unless there was some reason for changing it, which is generally obvious if we look for it. To

NORMAN ARCHES.

Triforium Arcade, Peterborough Cathedral, A.D. 1146.

This is the earliest example known of what is called Plate-tracery; this was soon followed by Bar-tracery in windows.

judge of the age of any building we must look at the general character of the work, and not seize upon some particular feature to ground any rule upon. The moldings are generally the safest guide, but even these sometimes require to be qualified by comparison with other parts.

The work is frequently quite as massive, and in all other respects of as early character, with the pointed arch as with the round one; they occur in Malmesbury Abbey Church, apparently in the work of Roger, bishop of Salisbury, A.D. 1115-1139, without any other apparent difference of character from the rest of the work. The pointed arch, taken by itself, is therefore no proof of the change of style, nor even of late work.

St. Cross Church, near Winchester, founded by Henry de Blois in 1136, has pointed arches; and the triforium has intersecting arcades, with the intervals left open as windows. To these may be added, Fountains Abbey, Yorkshire, founded in 1132: pointed arches occur in the early part of the work, which is of pure Norman character, and appears to have been built before the fire in 1140;—and Kirkstall Abbey, built between 1152 and 1182; here the work is of later character, but still pure Norman. All these are previous to the period of transition, and have not transitional moldings.

THE PIERS in the earlier period are either square solid masses of masonry, or recessed at the angles, in the same manner as the arches, or they are plain round massive pillars, with frequently only an impost of very simple character, but often with capitals. The round pillars are sometimes ornamented with a kind of fluting, as in the crypt at Canterbury, sometimes with a rude and shallow zig-zag pattern, as at Waltham Abbey, Durham, and Lindisfarne.

In the later period the pillars are in general not so massive as in the early part of the style, and are frequently ornamented with small shafts; and these as well as the pillars are sometimes banded, as at St. Peter's, Northampton.

The Capitals in early work are either plain cubical masses with the lower angles rounded off, forming a sort of rude cushion shape, as at Winchester, or they have a sort of rude volute, apparently in imitation of the Ionic, cut upon the angles; and in the centre of each face a plain square block in the form of the Tau cross is left projecting, as if to be afterwards carved: this remarkable feature is found in the chapel of the White Tower, London, in the early part of the crypt at Canterbury, at St. Nicholas, Caen, and other early work, but it has never been observed in late work.

The scolloped capital belongs to rather a later period than the plain cushion or the rude Ionic, and does not occur before the time of Henry I.; as at Stourbridge, Malmesbury, and Kirkstall. This form of capital was perhaps the most common of all in the first half of the twelfth century, and continued in use to the end of the Norman style.

The capitals were frequently carved at a period subsequent to their erection, as in the crypt at Canterbury (p. 37), where some of the capitals are finished, others half-finished, with two sides blank, and others not carved at all. In the early work at Westminster (p. 13), before mentioned, this is equally evident. At Castle Ashby, Northamptonshire, is the jamb of a Norman doorway with the pattern for the sculptor scratched upon it with the chisel, but never executed.

In later Norman work the capitals are frequently ornamented with foliage, animals, groups of figures, &c., in endless variety. The abacus throughout the style is the most characteristic member, and will frequently distinguish a Norman capital when other parts are doubtful. Its section is a square with the lower part chamfered off, either by a plain line or a slight curve; but as the style advanced it had other moldings added, and the whole are frequently so overlaid with ornament that it is difficult to distinguish the section (or profile) of its moldings.

NORMAN CAPITALS.

Grafton Underwood, c. A.D. 1160.

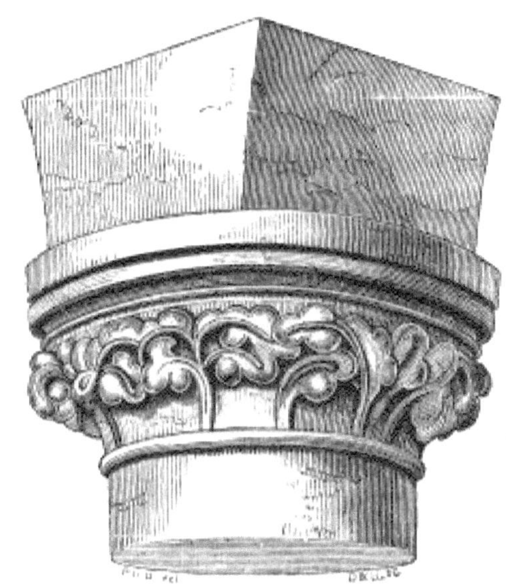

Woodford, c. A.D. 1180.

Canterbury, A.D. 1178.   Canterbury, A.D. 1178.

THE BASES are at first very simple, consisting merely of a quarter-round molding; then of two quarter-rounds, or two and a chamfer; or else of a round, or a chamfer and a quarter-round: as the style advanced they became more enriched, and the number of members more numerous: the earlier examples resemble the Tuscan, the later appear to be imitated from the Attic base. They always follow the form of the shaft or pillar, and stand upon a square pedestal or plinth; the angles of this square plinth being frequently filled up with some ornament, called foot-ornaments, or base ornaments: these increase in richness and boldness as the style advances, and their use was continued for some time in the subsequent style.

Canterbury Cathedral.   **Stoke Orchard, Gloucestershire.**

The Niches, or, Tabernacles, are small shallow recesses with round arches, frequently much enriched; they are chiefly placed over the doorways, and generally retain the figures which they were constructed to receive. These figures being executed in low relief upon the surface of the stone, were less liable to injury than the figures of the later styles, which are carved on separate stones and inserted. The most usual figure is that of Christ, distinguished by the cruciform nimbus. At Dorchester we have St. Peter with the key, under a semicircular arch, resting on cushion-capitals to twisted shafts, with molded bases. This example is from the font. The sculpture is at first very shallow, but becomes deeper as the style advances.

Niche with the Figure, Dorchester, Oxon.

THE MOLDINGS have been already mentioned in describing the doorways, where they are most abundantly used; they are, however, freely employed on all other arches, whether the pier-arches, or over windows, wall arcades, &c., and frequently also as horizontal strings or tablets. One of the most usual and characteristic Norman strings exactly resembles the abacus of the capital, or the impost of the pier, with a hollow chamfer under it; another is merely chamfered off above and below, forming a semi-hexagonal projection.

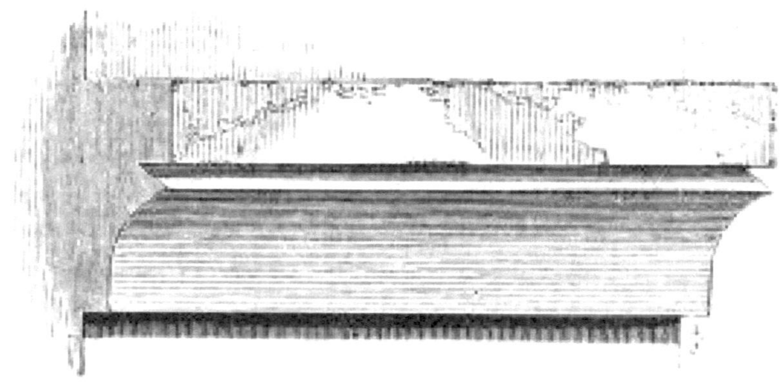

Norman Chamfer.

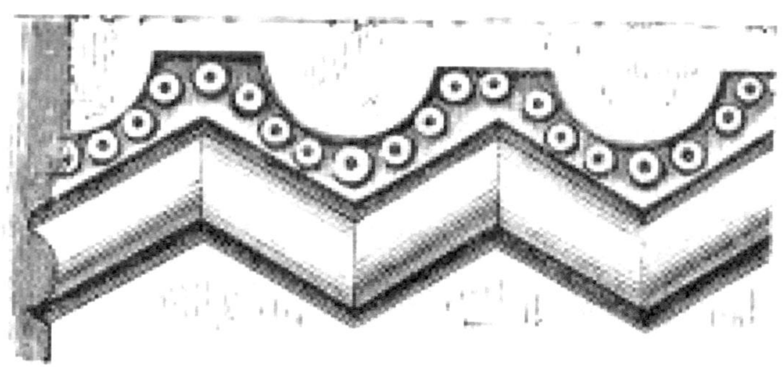

Chevron, or zig-zag, with Beads.

Norman ornaments are of endless variety; the most common is the chevron, or zig-zag, and this is used more and more abundantly as the work gets later; it is found at all periods, even in Roman work of the third century, and probably earlier, but in all early work it is used

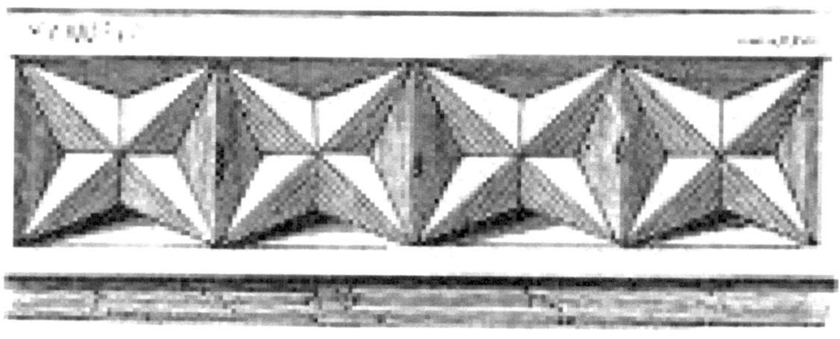

The Star.

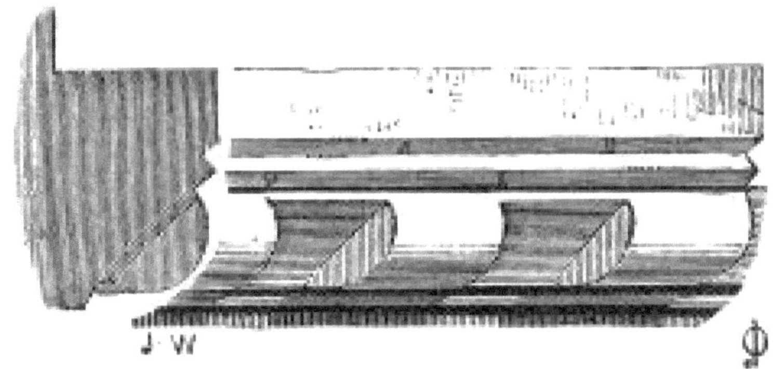

The Billet.

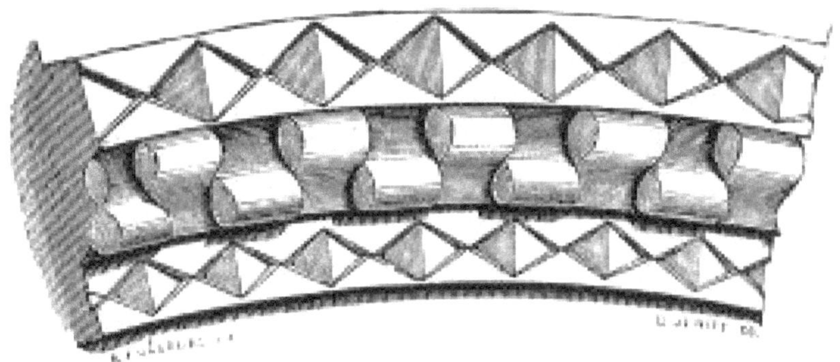

The Billet and Lozenge.

sparingly, and the profusion with which it is used in late work is one of the most ready marks by which to distinguish that the work is late. The sunk star is a very favourite ornament throughout the style; it occurs on the abacus of the capitals in the chapel of the White Tower, London, and at Herringfleet, Suffolk, and it seems to have been the fore-runner of the tooth-ornament. The billet is used in the early part of Peterborough, but discontinued in the later work, and does not often occur in late work. It is sometimes square, more frequently rounded, as in this example. The beak-head the cat's-head, the small medallions with figures, and the signs of the zodiac, all belong to the later Norman period. In the later Norman moldings a mixture of Byzantine character is seen on the ornaments, as at Durham.

Abacus and String.

Sculptured ornament made great progress during the twelfth century. We have seen by the testimony of Gervase that the chisel was not used in the "glorious choir of Conrad" at Canterbury, which was built between 1096 and 1130, and an examination of the old work proves the exactness of his statement; all the sculptured ornament on the old work is shallow, and such as could very well be executed with the axe, which is not a bad tool in the hands of a skilful workman, and is still commonly used in many parts of England and France. On comparing this early work at Canterbury with other early Norman buildings, it is plain that they all had their ornaments executed in the same manner: the chisel is only required for deep-cutting and especially undercutting, and that we do not find on any buildings of ascertained date before 1120. The chisel was used for carving in stone in Italy and the south of France at an earlier period, but not in Normandy nor the north of France much earlier than in England. After this usage was introduced, the workmen seem to have gloried in it, and revelled in it, and the profusion of rich Norman sculptured ornament in the latter half of the twelfth century is quite wonderful.

MOLDINGS AND CAPITALS.

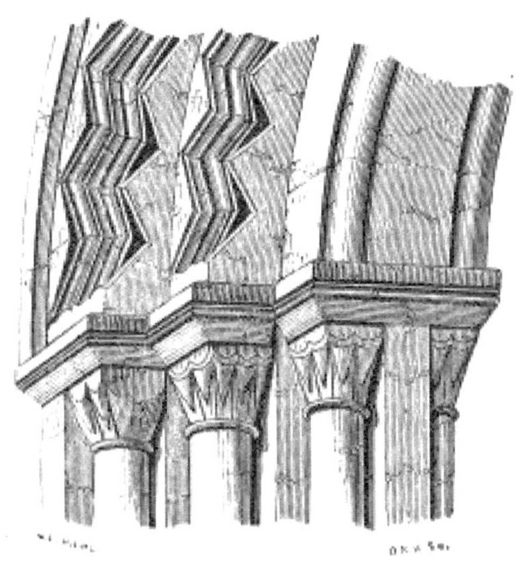 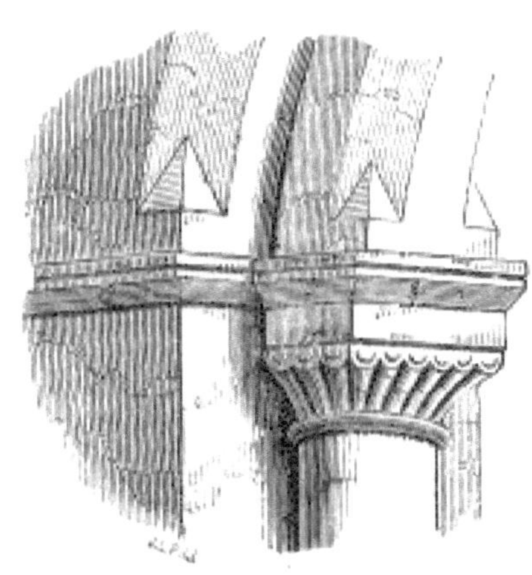

Brockworth, Gloucestershire.   Capital, Stoke Orchard, Gloucestershire.

It has been observed, that in the sculpture of the period of the late Norman style there is frequently a certain mixture of the Byzantine Greek character, brought home from the east by the Crusaders, who had returned. This is also one of the characteristics of the period of Transition.

THE CORBEL-TABLES are at first very plain, consisting merely of square blocks at intervals, carrying the beam on flat stones which support the roof, or with small arcs between them, or merely rude triangles, like the Anglo-Saxon arches; and these are sometimes continued in late work, as at Iffley, but in general, in late work the corbels are carved, and the small arcs more or less enriched. The buttresses are usually flat and plain in early examples, but have moldings on the angles in late examples.

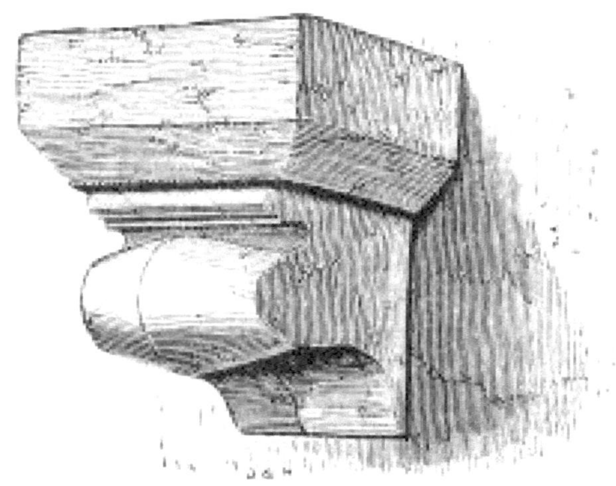

Norman Corbel.

Corbel-tables under the eaves of the roof are very abundant in late Norman and Transitional work, and are often proof that the walls are Norman, when this is not otherwise evident, later windows having been inserted. They are frequently square blocks of stone only, as if intended to be carved subsequently, when convenient, and this has never been done; more usually they are heads, or grotesque masks, as at Romsey.

THE PERIOD OF TRANSITION.

Corbel-tables, Romsey Abbey Church.

Of these two Corbel-tables, the upper one taken by itself would be Norman, c. A.D. 1160, and the lower one Early English; being both from the same church, they may both be classed as Transitional.

THE EARLIEST NORMAN VAULTS are quite plain, and of the barrel form, as in the chapel of the White Tower, London. In the next stage they have flat transverse arches only; they are then groined, but still without ribs: these plain groined vaults without ribs, over aisles or other narrow spaces, are often contemporaneous with the barrel vaults, and generally belong to the latter half of the eleventh century, or the beginning of the twelfth, as at Sherborne Castle, built by Roger, bishop of Salisbury, A.D. 1115-1139; at a later period ribs are introduced, at first square, then plain half-rounds, then molded, as in Peterborough Cathedral, A.D. 1117-1143, and they gradually change their form until they almost imperceptibly assume the character of Early English work.

The Norman architects did not venture to throw a vault over a wide space until very near the end of the style, and various contrivances were necessary for vaulting over spaces of unequal width, such as stilted arches, and horse-shoe arches, before the difficulty was solved by the use of the pointed arch. The absence of vaults over a wide space is a proof that the Norman was *not a continuation* of Roman work, as is sometimes assumed, but that there was always an interval of at least a century in which there were no masons.

EARLY NORMAN TURRETS are very rarely to be met with, but there are good examples at St. Alban's; at a later period they are frequent as stair-turrets, but have generally lost the original roof or capping; sometimes, as at Iffley, and Christ-church, Hampshire, they die into the tower below the corbel-table; in other instances, as at Bishop's Cleeve and Bredon, they are carried up above the parapet and terminate in pinnacles; they are sometimes round and sometimes square.

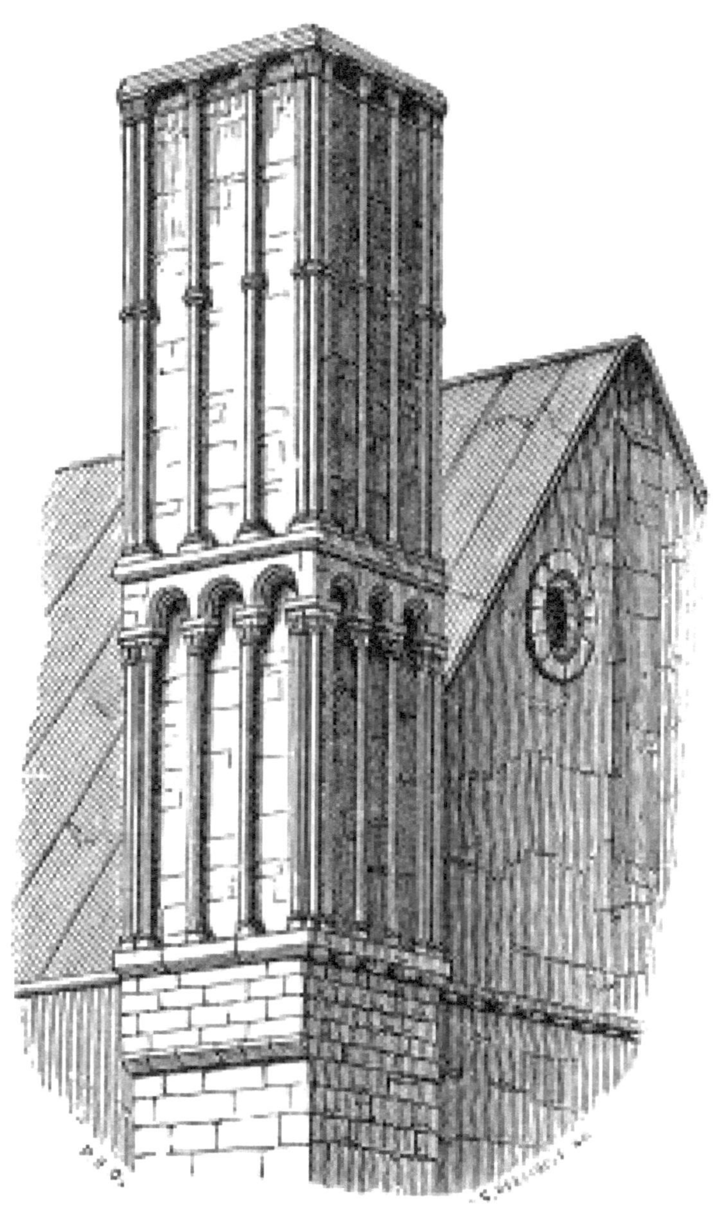

St. Cross, Winchester.

At St. Cross, Winchester, there is a remarkable example, something between a turret and a large square pinnacle, rising from the top of the side wall to the level of the front of the gables, and even above it.

NORMAN CENTRAL TOWERS are very low and massive, seldom rising more than a square above the roof, sometimes not so much, the ridge of the original roof, as shewn by the weather-table on the face of the tower, being only just below the parapet. These towers were intended to be, and without doubt originally were, covered by low wooden pyramidal roofs, resembling in appearance those which we find in some parts of Normandy of the same period, there executed in stone, on account of the abundance of the material, the facility with which it is worked, and the skill of the workmen.

When the towers are not placed over the centre of the church, but at the west end, it is remarkable that the later Norman towers are more massive and not so lofty as the early ones, as at Lincoln, Jarrow, &c., already described. They are comparatively low and heavy, sometimes diminishing by stages, and having buttresses of little projection on the lower parts. The belfry, or upper storey, has frequently been added in late Norman times upon the earlier towers. The belfry windows are generally double, and divided by a shaft. Towers of the pre-Norman period are generally remarkably tall, as at Deerhurst, one of the best dated examples.

THE ROUND TOWERS which are so abundant in Norfolk and Suffolk are frequently of the Norman period; some may be earlier, and others are certainly later; they are often so entirely devoid of all ornament or character, that it is impossible to say to what age they belong. The towers themselves are commonly, but not always, built of flint, sometimes of rough stone rubble, and are built round to suit the material, and to save the expense of the cut stone quoins for the corners which are necessary for square towers, and which often may not have been easy to procure in districts where building-stone has all to be imported. The same cause accounts for the frequent and long-continued use in the same districts of flat bricks or tiles for turning the arches over the doors and windows, which are either of Roman manufacture, or an imitation of the same form. Some good authorities think that the Roman form of flat bricks or tiles was long imitated in England.

Norman Round Tower, Norwich.

THE BUTTRESSES of this style were at first merely flat projections wholly devoid of ornament, and these are sometimes continued in late work; but in general, in late work there is a recess at the angle, in which a small shaft is inserted; the strings are sometimes continued round the buttresses and sometimes stop short at them, but in the latter case the buttresses have generally been added to strengthen the wall after it was erected, and are not part of the original work. In late Norman buildings the buttresses are sometimes square, and consequently have a much greater projection than the early flat buttresses. These square buttresses also have the moldings or shafts at the angles that the flat buttresses have not; an early Norman buttress never goes higher than the ground-floor, even when it is against a tower; at an angle, a flat buttress is placed on each side, nearly close to it.

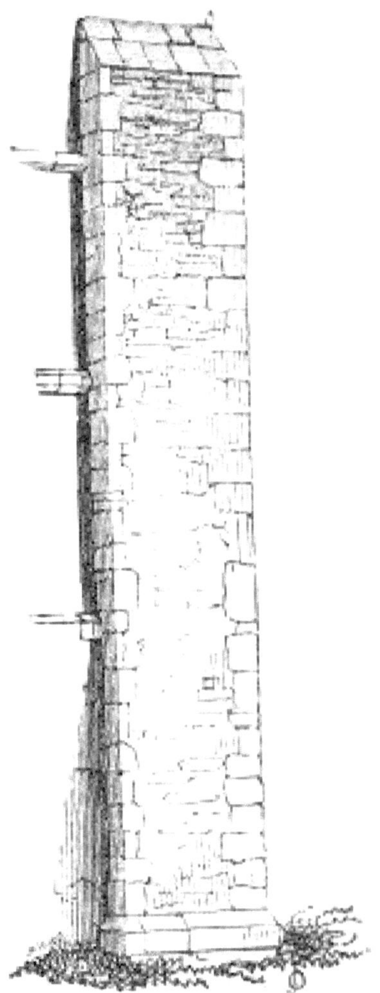

Flat Norman Buttress.

NORMAN PORCHES have in general very little projection, sometimes only a few inches, but the thickness of the wall allows the doorways to be deeply recessed; they are sometimes terminated by a gable, or pediment, as at St. Margaret-at-Cliffe, Kent, where the projection is so slight that it may be called either a doorway with a pediment over it, or a shallow porch. More frequently the projection ends in a plain set-off, in which case the appearance is that of a doorway set in a broad flat buttress. There are, however, a few porches which have as great a projection as those of the succeeding styles, and the sides of these are usually ornamented with arcades: the outer archway is of the same character as other doorways. At Sherborne and at Southwell Minster there are good examples of these porches.

But the square east end is the usual characteristic of the Anglo-Norman style; the apse is comparatively a rare feature in England. In the diocese of Laon in the north of France, the cathedral and a large number of the churches have square east ends, under the influence of an English bishop, who was a leading man there in the early part of the twelfth century. The small parish church of Cassington, Oxon, has a Norman chancel with a Norman vault also. At Iffley the original chancel was like that of Cassington—one square bay; another bay eastward of this is of the Early English style; both bays are vaulted. At Cassington, the whole of the walls of the church are Norman, and the lower part of the tower, but the belfry-storey and the spire are of *the Decorated style*. The thick abacus shews this corbel to be of quite early Norman character.

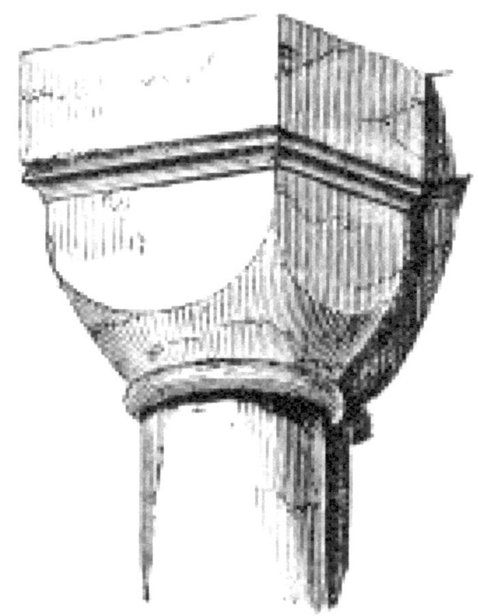

Norman Corbel, Cassington.

THE FRONTS, particularly the west fronts of Norman churches, are frequently of very fine composition, having generally deeply-recessed doorways, windows, and arcades, all covered with a profusion of ornament in the later period, as at Iffley, and at Nun-Monkton, p. 73.

THE APSE has been already mentioned as a characteristic of the Norman style. In England it is more frequently used in early than in late work, and is found at the east ends of the chancel and its aisles, and on the east side of the transepts; being, in fact, the places for altars, which were afterwards continued in the same situations, but either merely under windows in a flat wall, or under arched recesses which frequently remain in the transept wall, and are sometimes erroneously described as doorways.

Cassington, Oxon.

This is a small parish church, with a Norman chancel vaulted, remaining perfect; the walls of the nave are also Norman. The spire is an addition, in the Decorated style of the fourteenth century. (See the plan of this church at p. 39.)

The custom which has been mentioned of lengthening the churches eastwards, which commenced in the latter half of the twelfth century, was carried on vigorously in the thirteenth.

At Romsey there is an apse at the end of each of the aisles, not in the large central part.

Interior of a Norman Apse, Romsey Abbey, Hants, c. A.D. 1160.

PERIOD OF TRANSITION, A.D. 1160-1195.

WE have seen that during the half-century which intervened between 1125 and 1175 an immense number of churches were built or rebuilt in England, and that the art of building consequently made rapid progress, the work becoming every year better executed, more highly finished, and of lighter character, it being one of the characteristics of a good workman not to waste his material. In the early Norman period the masonry was very bad, and, to make the work secure, great masses of material were used; but at the period to which we have now arrived the masonry is as good as at any subsequent period, and the workmen were fast discovering the various modes of economizing their material. This practice, in combination with other causes, tended greatly to introduce the change of style, and to facilitate its ready and rapid adoption, in the generality of cases, when introduced. The custom of vaulting over large spaces, which was now being commonly adopted, and the difficulty of vaulting over spaces of unequal span, also without doubt contributed largely to the use of the pointed arch.

The capitals of the period are also very characteristic, and the gradual change may be clearly traced; at first the abacus-molding is very wide, and frequently only chamfered; a little later it is molded.

Capital of Window-shaft.

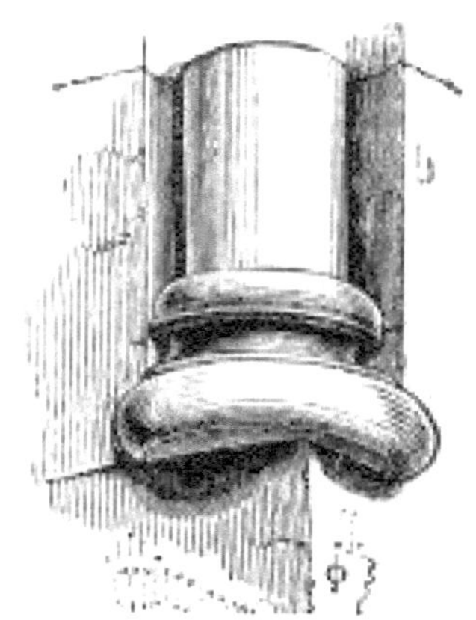

Base of Niche-shaft.

Nun-Monkton, Yorkshire.

The church of Nun-Monkton, in Yorkshire, is a very curious and fine example of this great period of Transition; the details are very boldly and well executed. The rich doorway by itself would be late Norman, whereas the niches on each side of it, and the three lancet-windows in the west front, are quite Early English. The square buttresses at the angles are late Norman, and the small square tower on the point of the gable has Norman corbel-tables. The heads of the windows in the tower are of the form sometimes called the shouldered-arch. The capitals of the window-shafts are a singular mixture of the two styles; the capital itself is well-molded Early English, and there is a hollow molding by the side of the shaft, with the tooth-ornament.

Nun-Monkton, Yorkshire, c. A.D. 1220.

In the work at Fountains Abbey already mentioned, the aisles are vaulted, and the width of the aisle being greater than the space between the pillars, it follows that each compartment, or bay, of the vault was not square, but oblong; the greater length being across the aisle, where we have the semicircular arch or arch-ribs to carry the vault, the narrower space being from pillar to pillar towards the choir: we have there the pointed arch, and thus we have a succession of semicircular arches down the length of the aisle, and a range of pointed arches towards the choir: and the same on each side. But although this may account for the use of the pointed arch, it is still quite distinct from the Gothic style; we have it at Fountains in pure Norman work half-a-century before we have the same arrangement again at Canterbury, in the work of William of Sens after the fire. Here, however, we have not only the pointed arch, but it is accompanied by a general change of style,—all the accessories are undergoing a rapid change. The moldings, the ornaments, the sculpture, and all other details are of a more highly finished and a lighter style. The triforium-arcade of Canterbury Cathedral is an excellent example, with the arches pointed and recessed, abacus well-molded, and foliage in the capitals.

Triforium Arcade, Canterbury Cathedral, A.D. 1178.

In this example the general arch is semicircular, while the two sub-arches under it are pointed, recessed, and square-edged, resting on coupled shafts with capitals of foliage, and molded bases on square plinths.

Canterbury, as has been pointed out, is the earliest and the best-authenticated example of the change of style in England which we possess, and it enables us to fix a precise date to this great change; it serves as a type for very many others which were being carried on simultaneously, or soon after. The contrast drawn by Gervase between the old church and the new one has been already quoted in describing the earlier Norman work, and need not here be repeated. It will be sufficient to say that the masonry and the sculpture in the new work are both excellent, and that the peculiar ornament known by the name of the 'tooth-ornament' occurs abundantly in the new work: the moldings, especially of the bases, are almost of pure Early English character.

The hall of Oakham Castle, Rutlandshire, built by Walkelin de Ferrers, between 1165 and 1191, is an excellent specimen of transitional work. It retains a great deal of the Norman character, but late and rich: the capitals are very similar to some of those at Canterbury, and more like French work than the usual English character; the tooth-ornament is freely introduced; the windows are round-headed within and pointed without, with good shafts in the jambs, and the tooth-ornament down each side of the shafts.

The triforium-arcade of St. Mary's, Shrewsbury, is also an excellent example; the arches are pointed, but square-edged only, and in the spandrel between the two lower arches is pierced with an open quatrefoil; it is also square-edged only, while the capitals have good foliage and a square abacus molded.

St. Mary's, Shrewsbury, c. A.D. 1180.

St. Frideswide Church, now Christ Church Cathedral, Oxford, is a fine example of late Norman and transitional work of early character. It was consecrated in 1180, and was probably building for about twenty years previously: the confirmation, by Pope Hadrian IV. (Breakspeare, the only English Pope), of the charters granting the Saxon monastery of St. Frideswide to the Norman monks was not obtained until 1158, and it is not probable that they began to rebuild their church until their property was secured. The Prior at this period was Robert of Cricklade, called Canutus, a man of considerable eminence, some of whose writings were in existence in the time of Leland. Under his superintendence the church was entirely rebuilt from the foundations, and without doubt on a larger scale than before, as the Saxon church does not appear to have been destroyed until this period. The design of the present structure is very remarkable; the lofty arched recesses, which are carried up over the actual arches and the triforium, giving the idea of a subsequent work carried over the older work; but an examination of the construction shews that this is not the case, that it was all built at one time, and that none of it is earlier than about 1160. In this church, the central tower is not square, the nave and choir being wider than the transepts, and consequently the east and west arches are round-headed, while the north and south are pointed: this would not in itself be any proof of transition, but the whole character of the work is late, though very rich and good, and the clerestory windows of the nave are pointed without any necessity for it, which is then a mark of transition.

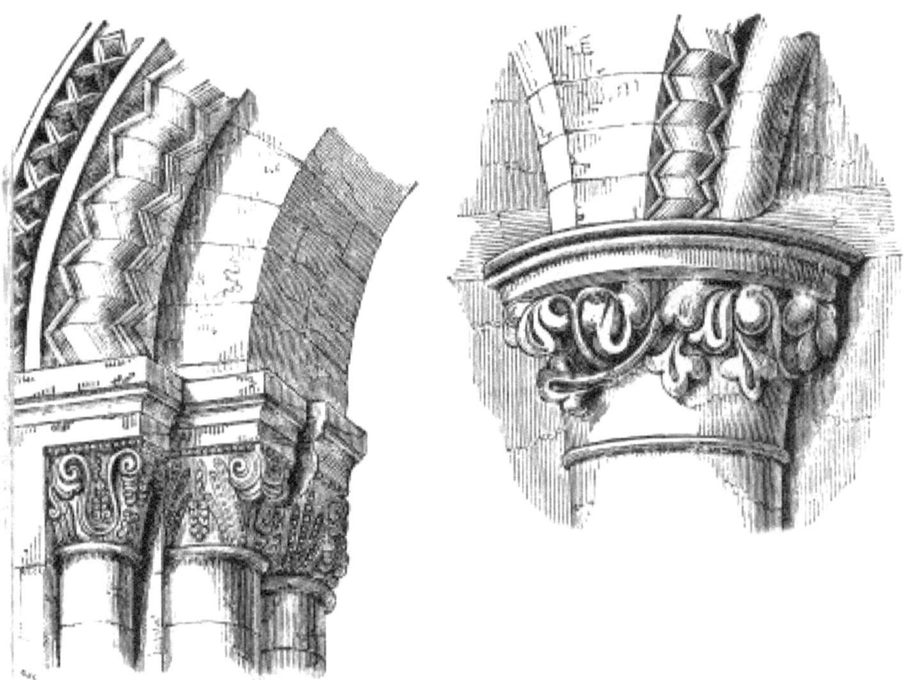

Romsey Abbey, c. A.D. 1180.

The tooth-ornament here shewn in the dripstone is usually a feature of the Early English style.

In this example, the foliage of the capitals and the molding of the abacus are quite Early English, while the zigzag molding of the arch would be Norman, if taken separately.

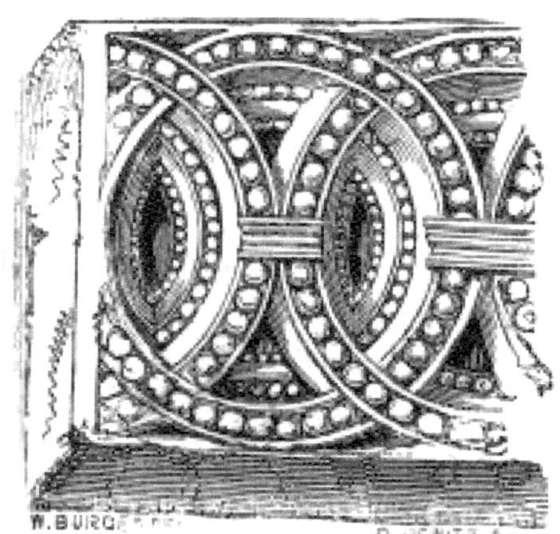

Westminster Abbey. Rich moldings from the original church, c. A.D. 1160.

Precisely the same design occurs in a part of Romsey Abbey Church, Hampshire, and very similar ones may be seen in other places: lofty arched recesses occur in Dunstable Priory Church, Bedfordshire, where Perpendicular windows have been inserted in the triforium, but the original design was the same.

The same mixture of the features that usually belong either to the Norman or to the Early English occur in all the details of the moldings, as at Canterbury, where we have the tooth-ornament of the Early English and the chevron or zigzag of the Norman style curiously mixed together. At Cuddesdon, again, in the molding of the fine west doorway, the same mixture occurs; the dripstone is the Early English round molding; then comes the chevron, standing out so boldly detached, that it almost becomes the tooth-ornament; and under that, on a smaller scale, the actual tooth-ornament occurs. The capital from St. Thomas' Church, Winchester, is equally curious; the abacus of a circular capital is, in fact, square-edged, with a round molding under it; and the foliage against the bell of the capital has the leaves curling over in the Early English fashion.

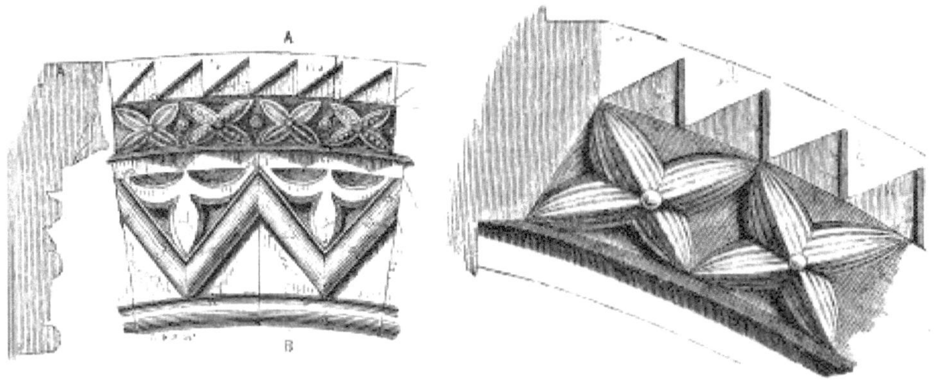

Moldings, Canterbury Cathedral, A.D. 1167.

These are good examples of the mixture of the chevron or zigzag with the tooth-ornament, not quite developed.

Cuddesdon, Oxon, c. A.D. 1180.   St. Thomas' Church, Winchester.

This is an interesting specimen of the latest Transition, almost Early English, but retains the square-edged abacus.

Examples of Domestic buildings of the houses of the twelfth century, in the Norman style, are rare, but we have still several remaining. At Lincoln there are two; one, on the hill, called the Jew's House, the other, in the lower town, was the house of St. Mary's Guild; and at Boothby Pagnel, in Lincolnshire, is a manor-house of this style: at Southampton are ruins of two houses, one called the King's House, formerly the custom-house, the other in a low part of the town, attached to the remains of the town wall; at Minster, in the aisle of Thanet, and at the Priory of Christchurch, in Hampshire, are houses which have belonged to monastic establishments; at Warnford, in the same county, are the foundations of a hall of this period; and in Farnham Castle, also in Hampshire, part of the great Norman hall remains, now converted into the servants' hall. At Appleton and Sutton Courtney, in Berkshire, are remains of manor-houses of this period; at Canterbury there are considerable remains of the monastic buildings of this century, among which is a fine external staircase with open arcades on each side; at Fountains Abbey, Yorkshire, there are extensive remains of the domestic buildings of pure Norman style; at Bury St. Edmund's, Suffolk, the house called Moyses' Hall, now used as the Bridewell, was probably the house of a wealthy Jew in the twelfth century.

THE EARLY ENGLISH STYLE.RICHARD I., JOHN,HENRY III.,A.D. 1189-1272.

THE great rapidity with which a decided change in the style and character of the work was taking place at this period, would appear almost incredible if it were not proved by so many instances, and especially by the well-authenticated account of Canterbury. After carefully noticing the great change which took place there during the ten years that the work was in progress, as recorded by Gervase, an eye-witness, and confirmed by Professor Willis, we shall not be much surprised to find some examples of pure Gothic work in the following ten years.

Canterbury was completed in 1184, and in 1185 St. Hugh of Grenoble, also called St. Hugh of Burgundy, was appointed bishop of Lincoln, and immediately began to rebuild his cathedral. It is therefore plain that this portion of the building was completed before 1200, and a careful examination enables us to distinguish clearly the work completed in the time of Bishop Hugh, which comprises his choir and the eastern transept, with its chapels. The present vaults of St. Hugh's choir, and of both the transepts, were introduced subsequent to the fall of the tower, which occurred in 1240.

The architecture in the north of Lincolnshire, and the south of Yorkshire, appears to have been a little in advance of any other in Europe at that period. St. Hugh's choir at Lincoln is the earliest building of the pure Gothic style, free from any mixture of the Romanesque, that has been hitherto found in Europe or in the world. The Oriental styles are not Gothic, though they helped to lead to it. The French Gothic has a strong mixture of the Romanesque with it down to a later period than the choir of Lincoln. St. Hugh of Lincoln certainly did not bring the Gothic style with him from his own country, Dauphiny, or from the Grande Chartreuse where he was educated, for nothing of the kind existed there at that period. Grenoble (the place from which St. Hugh was brought to England) and its neighbourhood was quite half-a-century behind England in the character of its buildings, in the time of Henry II. of England and of Anjou, in whose time this style was developed.

Nothing can well exceed the freedom, delicacy, and beauty of this work; the original arcade, of the time of St. Hugh, is of the same free and beautiful style as the additions of his successors. The foliage of the capitals is exquisitely beautiful, and though distinguished technically by the name of stiff-leaf foliage, because there are stiff stalks to the leaves, rising from the ring of the capital, the leaves themselves curl over in the most graceful manner, with a freedom and elegance not exceeded at any period.

St. Hugh's Choir, South Aisle, Lincoln, A.D. 1195.

This is an unusually perfect example, with the original ornaments, of the earliest
building of pure Gothic, free from Romanesque or Norman.

Beverley Minster, Yorkshire.

The moldings are also as bold and as deep as possible, and there is not a vestige of Norman character remaining in any part of the work. The crockets arranged vertically one over the other behind the detached marble shafts of the pillars, are a remarkable and not a common feature, which seems to have been in use for a few years only; it occurs also in the west front of Wells Cathedral, the work of Bishop Jocelyn, a few years after this at Lincoln; or perhaps under him, of Hugh de Wells.

Beverley Minster, Yorkshire, c. A.D. 1230.

Possibly the double arcade at Beverley (page 86) originated in the same manner as that at Lincoln, in St. Hugh's choir, from the necessity for thickening the wall to make it carry a stone vault, and at the same time, a reluctance to hide the arcade in the original wall. At Lincoln they are clearly of two periods, though still in the same style. At Glasgow Cathedral, which has one of the finest crypts in existence, the work was commenced by Bishop Joceline in 1195.

The choir and transepts of Rochester Cathedral were also building soon after this time, and are a very beautiful and remarkable example of Early English. The architect was William de Hoo, first sacristan, then prior, and there is some reason to believe that he is the same person as William the young Englishman, who assisted William of Sens after his fall from the scaffold at Canterbury, and completed the work there. A young man at Canterbury in 1185, able to carry on and complete such a work, may very well have become the architect on his own account of the daughter church of Rochester in 1201-1227, and there is great resemblance in style between Rochester and the later work at Canterbury.

THE DOORWAYS are generally pointed or trefoiled, but sometimes round-headed, and in small doorways frequently flat-headed, with the angles corbelled in the form called the square-headed trefoil, or the shouldered arch. This form of opening is frequently called the Carnarvon arch, from its being so generally used in that castle; but it is often of earlier date, though it also continued in use for a long period. The rather happy name of the 'shouldered arch' was given to it; strictly speaking, it is not an arch at all, and the shouldered lintel, or the corbelled lintel, would perhaps be more correct.

The Dean's Door in the Cloister, Westminster Abbey, A.D. 1250.

A very rich and rather late example of this style.

The Priest's Door, Irchester, Northants.

The round-arched doorways may readily be distinguished by their moldings; they are commonly early in the style, but by no means always so: segmental arches also occur. Trefoil-arches are characteristic of this style.

West Door and shallow Porch of the Chapel of the Bishop's Palace, Wells.

The chapel of the Bishop's Palace at Wells is altogether a remarkable example of the latter part of this style; it was originally built by Bishop Jocelyn in the early part of the thirteenth century, but much altered and partly rebuilt towards the end of it. The west doorway is a very remarkable one, the arch itself being cinquefoiled, with a semicircular dripstone.

THE PORCHES are frequently shallow, as in the example from Wells, p. 91, but there are many fine porches of the usual projection; these have sometimes very lofty gables, as at Barnack, Northamptonshire. The outer doorways are often much enriched with moldings and shafts of great depth, and the walls are ornamented on the inside with arcades and tracery.

Stanton Harcourt, East End, with triple Chancel-window, c. A.D. 1250.

A good example of the east front of a parish church of the earlier part of this style.

"Early English Buildings are readily distinguished from those of the Norman period by their comparative lightness, their long, narrow, lancet-shaped, pointed windows, their boldly projecting buttresses and pinnacles, and the acute pitch of the roof. Internally, we have pointed arches supported on slender and lofty pillars, which are frequently formed of a number of shafts connected at intervals by bands. One of these shafts is frequently carried up to the springing of the roof, where it ramifies in various directions to form the ribs of the vaulting, which have now lost the heaviness of the Norman period and are become light and elegant. The whole character of the building is changed, and instead of the heavy masses and horizontal lines of the Norman style, we have light and graceful forms and vertical lines."

The rapidity with which the change of style took place has been pointed out, and the complete character of the change, which was developed as fully in some of the earliest buildings of the new style as in the latest. New ideas and a new life seem to have been given to architecture, and the builders appear to have revelled in it even to exuberance and excess, and it was necessary afterwards, in some degree, to soften down and subdue it. At no period has "the principle of verticality" been so completely carried out as in the Early English style, and even in some of the earliest examples of it.

The characteristic of lancet-windows applies only to the early part of the style, from A.D. 1190 to about A.D. 1220 or 1230, after that time circles in the head of the windows of two or more lights came in, and the circles became foliated by about A.D. 1230, and from that time to 1260 or 1270, when the Decorated style began to come into fashion.

The Windows in the earlier examples are plain, lancet-shaped, and generally narrow, as at Stanwick and Bakewell; sometimes they are richly molded within and without, but frequently have nothing but a plain chamfer outside and a wide splay within.

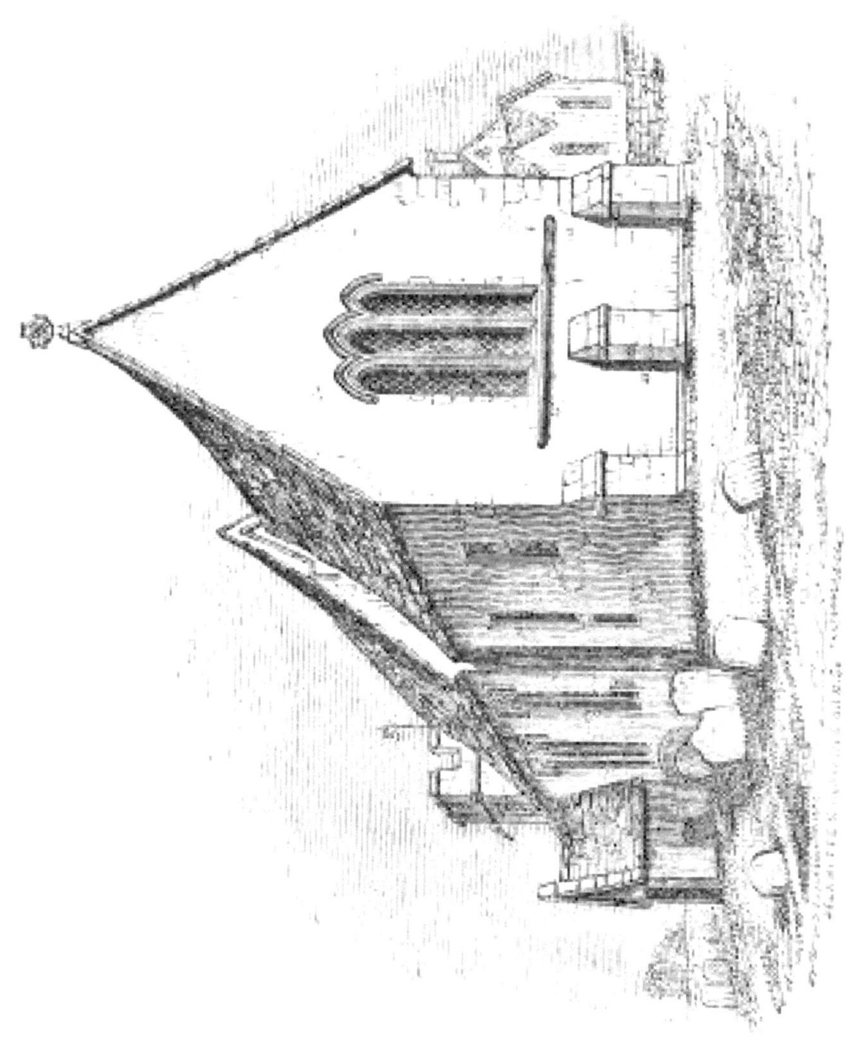

South-east View of Cowley Church, Oxon.

Square-headed windows are not at all uncommon in this style, more especially in houses; they frequently occur also in churches, as in the small church of Cowley, near Oxford. Sometimes, when the central

Stanwick, Northants, c. A.D. 1220.

An unusually narrow lancet-window, with very wide splay, and coupled shafts in the inner arch.

Bakewell, Derbyshire.

A good example of the hood-mold over the inner arch (or scoinson-arch).

opening is square-headed, there is an arch or a dripstone in the form of an arch over it, with the space or tympanum filled up with ornament, as at Ringstead, Northants. But this arch over the square head is frequently wanting, and these simple square-headed windows of the thirteenth century, which are very common, especially in castles, are often mistaken for Perpendicular work of the fifteenth.

In the Early English style we have, in the later examples, tracery in the heads of the windows, but it is almost invariably in the form of circles, either plain or foliated, and is constructed in a different manner from genuine Decorated tracery. At first the windows have merely openings pierced through the solid masonry of the head, the solid portions thus left gradually becoming smaller and the openings larger, until the solid parts are reduced to nearly the same thickness as the mullions; but they are not molded, and do not form continuations of the mullions until we arrive at real Decorated tracery. This kind of tracery was called by Professor Willis *plate* tracery; being, in fact, a plate of stone pierced with holes: it is extensively used in Early French work. The more usual kind of tracery, as at Winchester and Romsey, is called by Professor Willis *bar* tracery, to distinguish it from the earlier kind. These terms are so expressive and convenient that they are now generally adopted.

WINDOWS.

Romsey Abbey, c. A.D. 1250.	St. John's, Winchester, c. A.D. 1260.
A very rich example, with beautiful foliage on the inner arch, and shafts to that and to the mullions.	This belongs to the later division of the style, with foliated circles in the tracery of the window, and shafts to the inner arch.

The Arches are frequently, but not always, acutely pointed, and in the more important buildings are generally richly molded, as in Westminster Abbey, either with or without the tooth-ornament, as the arches at York Minster. It has been already observed that the form of the arch is never a safe guide to the date or style of a building—it depended much more on convenience than anything else; the moldings are the most safe guide: for instance, the arches of the nave of Westminster Abbey are of the same form as those of the choir and transepts, yet they were built by Sir Richard Whittington, (better known by the story of his cat), in the fifteenth century, and their moldings belong distinctly to that period. In plain parish churches the arches are frequently without moldings, merely recessed and chamfered; the only character being in the capitals and bases, or perhaps in the hoodmolds, though these also are sometimes wanting.

Very acute arches are generally the earliest, but this cannot be relied upon as a rule; an Early English arch is sometimes very flat, being made *within* an existing Norman one, which was semicircular, owing to some change of plan, as in the Lady Chapel of Oxford Cathedral; and similar examples are not uncommon, when the convenience of the construction calls for flat arches.

Wall Arcade in Chapel of Choir, Westminster Abbey, A.D. 1260.

THE PILLARS are of various forms—round or octagonal in small and plain churches, and these not unfrequently alternate; in richer work they are usually clustered; but the pillar most characteristic of the style is the one with detached shafts, which are generally of Purbeck marble, frequently very long and slender, and only connected with the central shaft by the capital and base, with or without one or two bands at intervals. These bands are sometimes rings of copper gilt, as in the choir of Worcester Cathedral, and were sometimes necessary for holding together the slender shafts of Purbeck marble.

Another peculiarity consists of the Foliage, which differs considerably from the Norman: in the latter it has more or less the appearance of being imitated from that of the Classic orders, while in this it is entirely original. Its essential form seems to be that of a trefoil leaf, but this is varied in such a number of ways that the greatest variety is produced. It is used in cornices, the bosses of groining, the moldings of windows and doorways, and various other places, but particularly in capitals, to which it gives a peculiar and distinctive character. The foliage of these capitals is technically called "Stiff-leaf foliage," but this alludes only to the stiff stem or stalk of the leaf, which rises from the ring of the capital; the foliage itself is frequently as far removed from stiffness as any can be, as for instance in the capitals of Lincoln. The stiff stalk is, however, a ready mark to distinguish the Early English capital from that of the succeeding style.

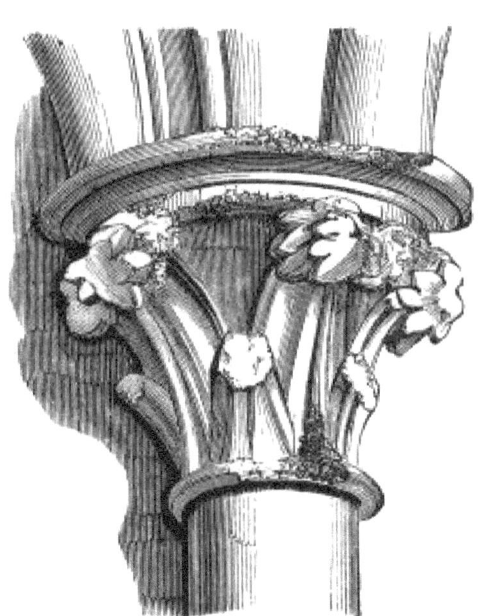

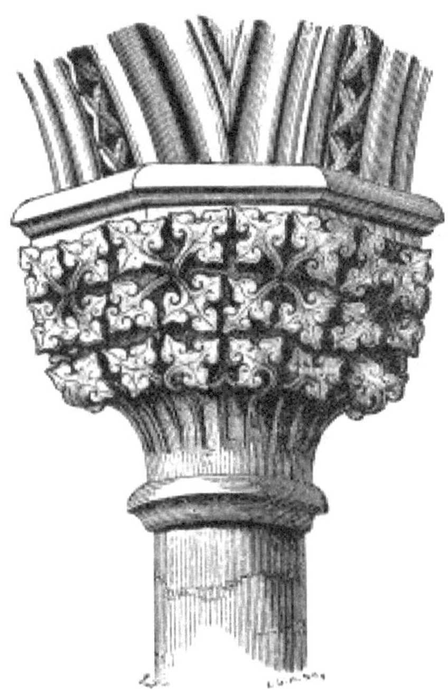

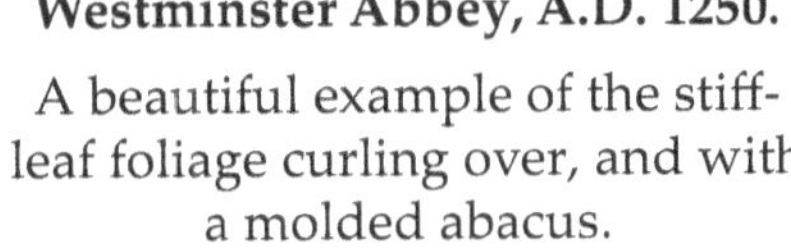

Westminster Abbey, A.D. 1250.

A beautiful example of the stiff-leaf foliage curling over, and with a molded abacus.

Beverley, Yorkshire, c. A.D. 1260.

An unusually rich example, with profuse foliage; also an abacus, with the roll-molding.

Capital of Shaft, A.D. 1250.   **Capital at the North-west Angle
of the Cloister.**

WESTMINSTER ABBEY.

We must bear in mind, however, that foliage is by no means an essential feature of the Early English style; many of our finest buildings, such as Westminster
Abbey, have their capitals formed of a plain bell reversed, with moldings round
the abacus, like rings put upon it, and round the neck.

BASES.

Choir, Canterbury, A.D. 1178.

Corona, Canterbury, A.D. 1184.

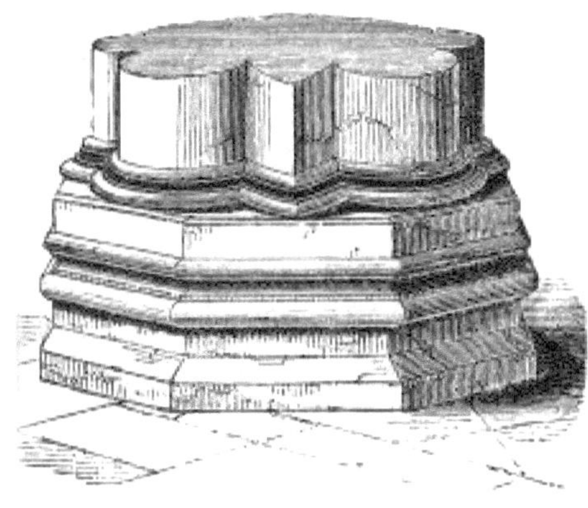

Beverley Minster, A.D. 1220.

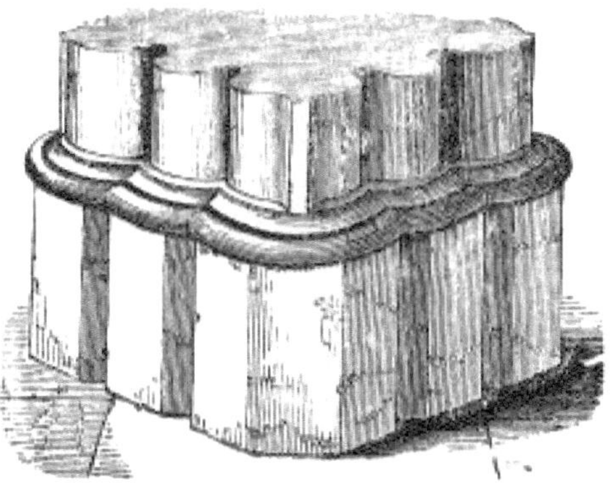

Selby, Yorkshire, A.D. 1260.

THE BASES generally consist of two rounds, the lower one the largest, both frequently filleted, with a deep hollow between placed horizontally, as at Canterbury; but in later examples this hollow is not found, its place being filled up with another round molding, as at Selby, p. 103. They frequently approach in contour to the Grecian attic base, and the ogee is sometimes employed, as Rickman observed with his usual accuracy.

The deeply-cut moldings in bases of this style will frequently hold water, and this is sometimes called one of the characteristics of the style; but it is not a good one, because it is not easy to decide whether a particular base will hold water or not. These bases are frequently stilted, that is, the principal molding is raised a foot or two from the floor, and the space is sometimes plain; in some instances an additional molding is introduced; again, in other instances some foliage, or wavy-line molding, as in the choir at Canterbury, which is the earliest example of the style, and chiefly transitional. This stilted part, or plinth, is sometimes square; this is generally in the earlier examples: in other cases it is polygonal, or round, with an ornamental molding upon it, going round the whole pier, in addition to the base-moldings of the separate shafts of the cluster of four, five, or six, that form the piers, as at Beverley, Canterbury, and Selby.

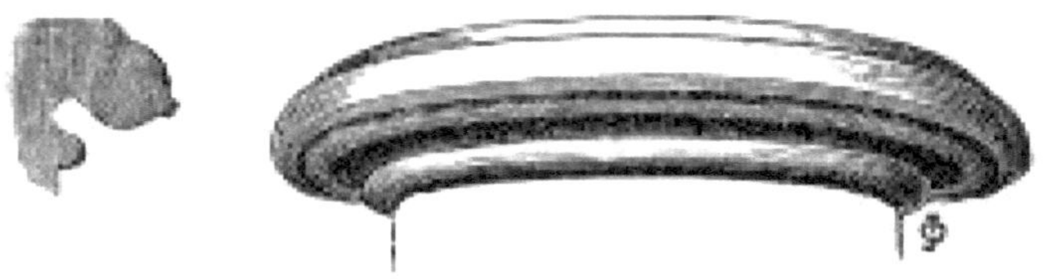

Abacus with round and hollow molding.

In pure Early English work, the upper member of the capital, called the ABA-CUS, is circular, and consists, in the earlier examples, simply of two rounds, the upper one the largest, with a hollow between them; but in later examples the moldings are frequently increased in number and filleted. The general use of the circular abacus is peculiar to England and Normandy; even in the best early French work, of the Royal Domain, the abacus is generally square; and as there can be no doubt that the round abacus is more consistent with pure Gothic work, the square one belonging more properly to the Classic styles, this circumstance is a strong argument in favour of the greater purity of English Gothic. Generally, also, the MOLDINGS are much more numerous and much richer in English work than in foreign work of the same period, as has been said.

One of the chief characteristics of the Early English style consists in the MOLD-INGS, which differ essentially from these of the Norman; for while those consisted chiefly of squares with round moldings on the angles, or with the angles chamfered off, in the Early English they are chiefly bold rounds, with equally bold and deeply cut hollows, which produce a strong effect of light and shade. In many of the earlier examples the square profile of the recessed Norman arch is retained, and the moldings are cut chiefly on the angles; but as the style advances this squareness is lost, and the moldings appear to be cut on a chamfer, or sloping surface, as at Little Addington and Denford, Northants, and none of the plain square masonry remains, the whole being worked up into rich suites of moldings, separated only by deep hollows. In the later examples a peculiar molding called the roll[4] mold-ing, is used; and it was still more used in the succeeding, or Decorated style, and is often considered one of the marks of that style. The fillet was now used profusely on the rounds; one, two, or sometimes three fillets being cut on a single molding, as in the choir of the Temple Church, London, thus giving a very different though

[4] Sometimes called the *scroll* molding, but *roll* is the correct term, from the close resemblance to a roll of parchment with the edge overlapping.

still beautiful character to them; but this always shews a tendency of transition to the next style.

Throughout the Early English period there is an ornament used in the hollow moldings which is as characteristic of this style as the zigzag is of the Norman; this consists of a small pyramid, more or less acute, cut into four leaves or petals meeting in the point, but separate below, as in Chester Cathedral. When very acute, and seen in profile, it may be imagined to have somewhat the appearance of a row of dog's-teeth, and from this it has been called the "dog-tooth ornament," or by some the shark's-tooth ornament, more commonly the "TOOTH-ORNA-MENT." It is used with the greatest profusion on arches, between clustered shafts, on the architraves and jambs of doors, windows, piscinas, and indeed in every place where such ornament can be introduced. It is very characteristic of this style, and begins quite at the commencement of the style, as in St. Hugh's work at Lincoln; for though in the Norman we find an approach to it, in the Decorated various modifications of it occur; still the genuine tooth-ornament may be considered to belong exclusively to the Early English.

MOLDINGS.

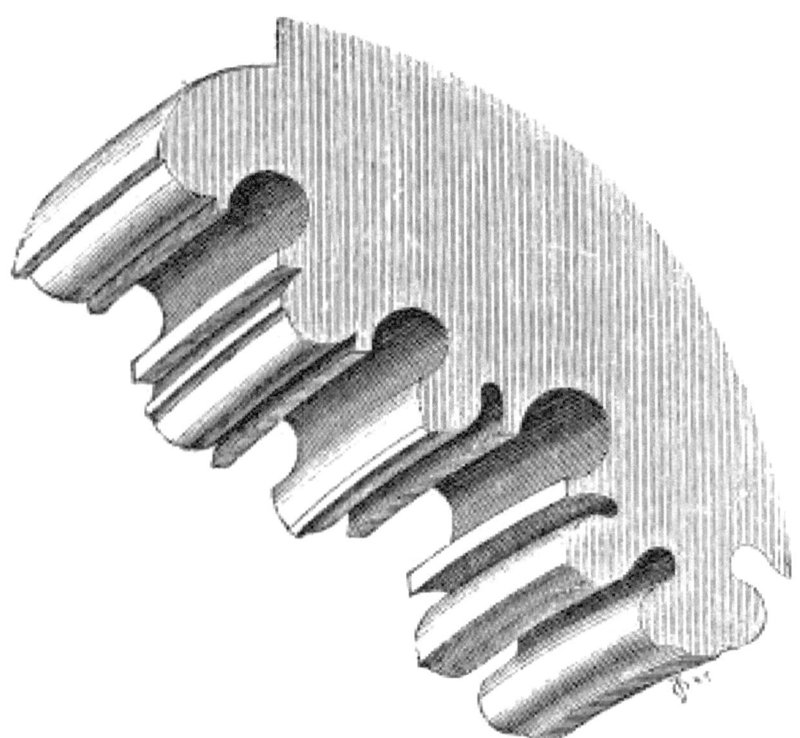

Little Addington, Northants, c. A.D. 1250.

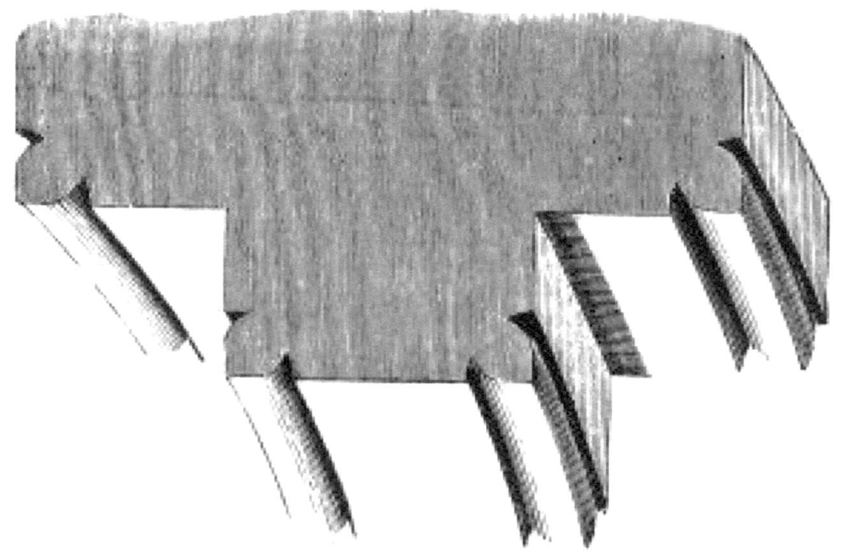

Chancel-arch, Haseley, Oxon.

Chester Cathedral.

The natural use and the profusion of moldings in the English buildings of the thirteenth century is considered as one of the proofs of the English origin of the Gothic style. The French imitated it rapidly, but in a cheaper manner, and their buildings are, on the whole, not quite equal to ours, that is, taking into account both exterior and interior. The profuse suites of moldings so common in English doorways and arches, are almost unknown in France: some things they developed more rapidly than we did, but in the moldings they were behind us.

THE VAULTS are distinguished from the Norman by their greater boldness, and from succeeding styles by their greater simplicity, as at Salisbury. In the earlier examples there are ribs on the angles of the groins only; at a later period the vaulting becomes more complicated, as at Westminster. There is a longitudinal rib, and a cross rib along the ridge of the cross vaults, and frequently also an intermediate rib on the surface of the vault. The bosses are rare at first, more abundant afterwards: they are generally well worked and enriched with foliage.

Early English vaults are sometimes of wood only, as in York Minster, and at Warmington, Northamptonshire, and the cloisters at Lincoln. A vault is, in fact, a ceiling, having always an outer roof over it; and there is no necessity for its being of stone, although it is obviously better that it should usually be so, as a security against fire, which was the chief motive for the introduction of stone vaults. It generally is so; the chapel of St. Blaise, or the old revestry, in Westminster Abbey, is an excellent example little known. The rather incorrect use of the word 'roof' by Mr. Rickman, as applied to vaults, has led to some confusion of ideas on this subject.

There is a marked distinction in the construction of Gothic vaults in England and France. In England, from the earliest period, each stone is cut to fit its place, in France the stones are cut square or rather oblong, as in the walls, and only wedged out by the thickness of the mortar at the back in the joints. The English system is far more scientific, but also far more costly; the French system is infinitely more economical of labour, and consequently of expense.

Chapel of St. Blaise, Westminster Abbey, A.D. 1250.

From this cause stone vaults are far more common in France than in England. From this cause also fan-tracery vaulting is peculiar to England, and it begins, in principle, as early as in the cloister of Lincoln, c. A.D. 1220, where the vault is of wood, but the springings are of stone, and cut to fit the ribs of the wooden vault.

The beautiful vaulted chambers in the Bishop's Palace at Wells are part of the original work, begun in the time of St. Hugh, and finished under his immediate successor, Jocelyn. Grand chambers as these now appear to us, they were originally cider-cellars under the great hall, which was very lofty, and had a wooden roof only, which still exists, though in a very neglected state, and too much dilapidated by alterations of various periods to be left visible. It was concealed by a beautiful plaster-ceiling by Bishop Bagot in 1850; the fine vaulted chambers of these cellars [see p. 113] are now used as the dining-room of the bishop's family and their guest-chamber, and part of them, separated by a wall, is the entrance-hall. This latter feature is an original arrangement, not a modern alteration, as some have supposed; it served as a passage to the bishop's chapel from the other part of the house, and from the offices also.

Vaulted Chambers of the Bishop's Palace, Wells, A.D. 1195-1210.

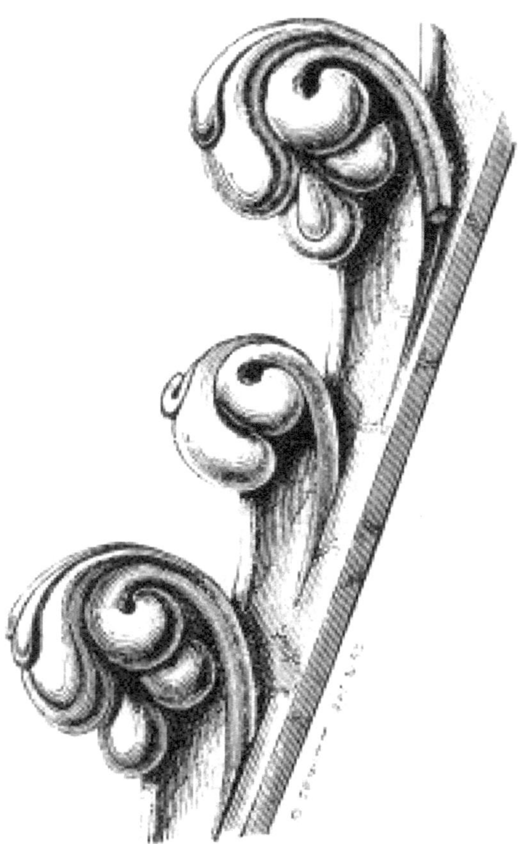

Crockets, Tomb of Abp. Walter Grey, York Cathedral, A.D. 1255.

The ornaments so well known by the name of Crockets were first introduced in this style. The name is taken from the shepherd's crook, adopted by the bishops as emblematical of their office. They occur at Lincoln, in St. Hugh's work, the earliest example of this style, and are there used in the unusual position of being in a vertical line between the detached shafts. They are found in the same position also in the beautiful work of the west front of Wells. Afterwards they were used entirely on the outside of pediments, or in similar situations, projecting from the face of the work or the outer surface of the molding, as in the very beautiful tomb of Archbishop Walter Grey, in York Cathedral; and they continued in use in the subsequent styles, although their form and character gradually change with the style.

EARLY ENGLISH ORNAMENTS GABLE CROSSES.

Warkton.

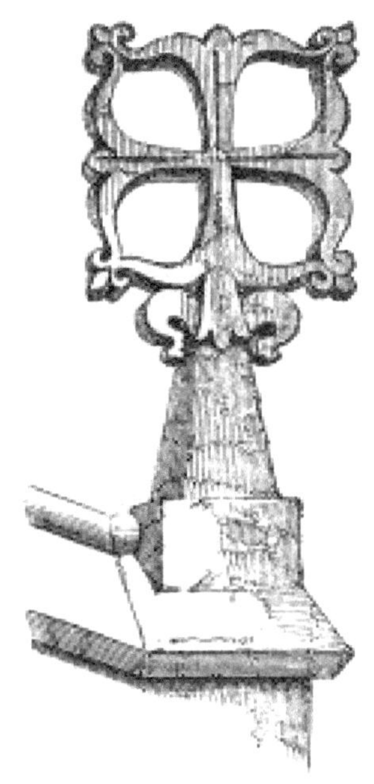

Cranford St. John.

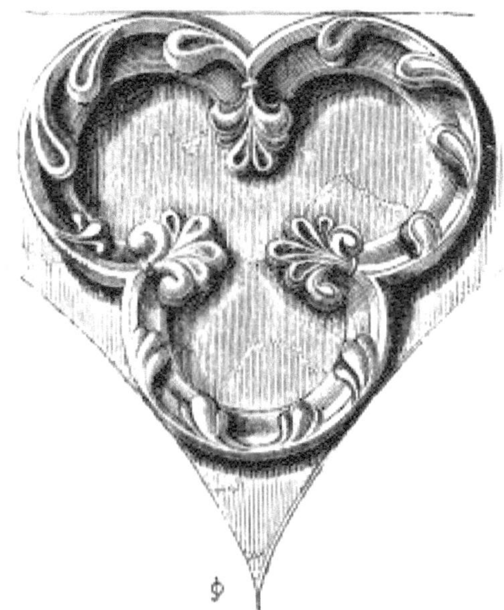

Panel and Cusp, Raunds.

The Buttresses, instead of being, as in the last style, mere strips of masonry slightly projecting from the wall, have now a very bold projection, and generally diminish upwards by stages, terminating either in a pedimental head, or gable, as at Wrington, Northants, or in a plain sloping set-off, as in the lower part of those at Higham Ferrars. The angles are frequently broadly chamfered, and sometimes ornamented with shafts, either solid or detached. On towers the buttresses are frequently carried up to the second storey, as at Ravensthorpe, p. 123.

The pinnacles terminating the buttresses are at first sometimes square, as at Bishop's Cleeve, Gloucestershire, which is of transitional Norman character: they are not very numerous in the Early English style, and often consist merely of an octagonal shaft with a pyramidal capping; afterwards, particularly in large buildings, they are either round or octagonal, with shafts at the angles, sometimes supporting small arches, and terminating in a plain conical capping ending in a bunch of foliage or other ornament as a finial, as at Peterborough.

The Flying Buttress now becomes a prominent feature in large buildings. It is often found in Norman work, but concealed under the roof of the

EARLY ENGLISH BUTTRESSES.

Wrington, c. A.D. 1220.   **Higham Ferrars, c. A.D. 1220.**

triforium, as at Durham, Winchester, and many other fine Norman buildings; but in this style it is carried up higher, and is altogether external, spanning over the roof of the aisle, and carrying the weight and consequent thrust of the vault over the central space obliquely down to the external buttresses, and so to the ground, as in St. Hugh's choir at Lincoln, beforementioned as the earliest example of this style. There is a very fine example of a compound flying buttress at Westminster Abbey, which supports the vaults of the choir, the triforium, and the aisles, and carries the thrust of the whole over the cloister to the ground. But they did not become common until after this period. There is a marked difference between the flying buttresses of English buildings and those of French work of the same time; the English are far more elegant; large French buildings often appear as if they were surrounded by a scaffolding of stone.

THE FRONTS of Early English buildings before the introduction of tracery, and consequently before the use of large windows, have a very peculiar appearance, very different from those of the preceding or succeeding styles. In small churches a common arrangement is to have either three lancet windows in the west front, as at Stanton Harcourt, Oxon, p. 92, or two with a buttress between them at the west end, as at Elsfield, Oxon; but in both cases there is frequently over them a quatrefoil or small circular window foliated, or sunk panels of the same form, but not pierced as windows. In large buildings there are frequently two or three tiers of lancet windows, and a rich circular window in the gable above.

South-west View of Elsfield Church, Oxon.

Early English Towers are in general more lofty than the Norman, and are readily distinguished by their buttresses, which have a greater projection. In the earlier examples an arcade is frequently carried round the upper storey, some of the arches of which are pierced for windows, as at Middleton Stoney, Oxon: but in later buildings the windows are more often double, and are frequently very fine compositions, as at Ravensthorpe, Northants. The tower generally terminates in a Spire, which in some districts, especially in Northamptonshire, does not rise from within a parapet, but is of the form usually called a broach spire, of which there are several varieties. In other districts the towers are terminated by original parapets; these probably had wooden spires rising within the parapet, which occasionally but rarely remain, and are a good feature, as at Ilton, Somerset. Pinnacles are sometimes inserted at the angles, and produce a very good effect.

The spire is generally a very fine feature of an Early English church; some great architects have gone so far as to say that a tower is never complete without one, but that is going too far. There *may have been wooden* spires on such towers as those of Middleton Stoney and Ravensthorpe, but we have no evidence of it; there are no *squinches* to carry a spire.

Middleton Stoney, Oxon, c. A.D. 1240. Ravensthorpe, Northants, c. A.D. 1260.

The East End is almost invariably square in Early English work, as at Cowley,

Oxon, p. 94, although we have a few examples of the apsidal termination, generally a half-octagon, or half-hexagon, as in Westminster Abbey, and several other large churches. In the small parish churches this form is very rare: an example occurs at Tidmarsh, near Pangbourne, Berks, an elegant little structure, the roof of which has been carefully restored.

THE CORBEL-TABLES sometimes consist, as in the earlier period, merely of blocks supporting a straight, projecting course of stone which carries the front of the parapet; but more commonly, especially as the style advanced, small trefoil arches are introduced between the corbels, and these become more enriched and less bold, until, in the succeeding style, this feature is altogether merged in the cornice moldings.

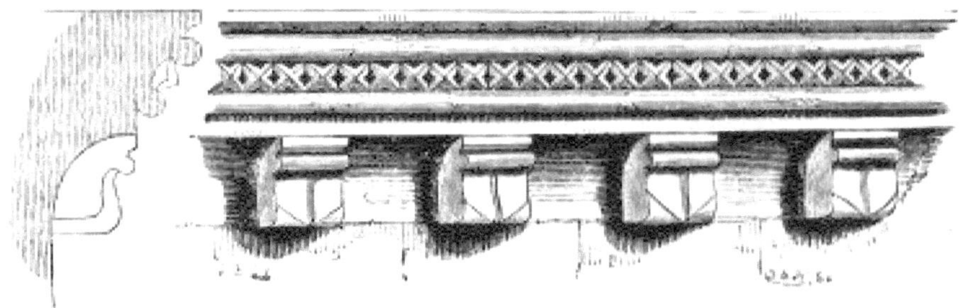

Corbel-table, Beverley Minster.

In the latter part of this style great liberty was allowed to the carvers, and much ingenuity displayed in

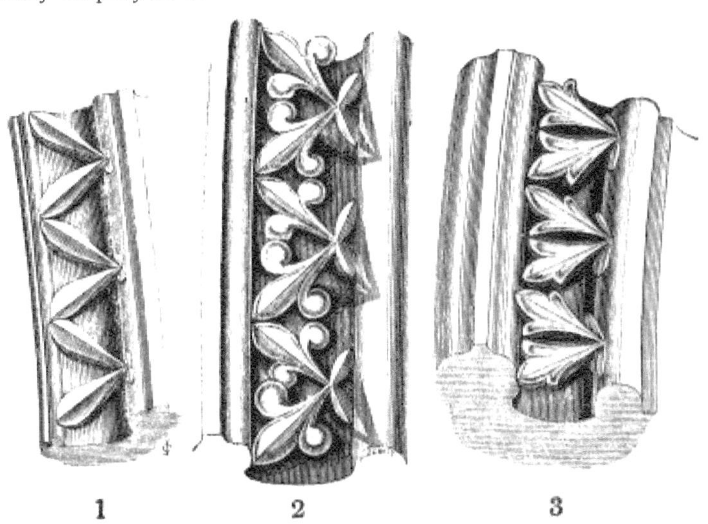

1   2   3

Varieties of the Tooth-ornament, Binham Priory, Norfolk.

the variety of ornament that was introduced; although always conventional. For instance, in the description of ornament which goes by the general name of "tooth-ornament," for want of a better, there is a singular variety; even in the church of Binham alone, there are three varieties of what is called the tooth-ornament, not bearing much resemblance to each other, though all elegant. One has the knobs on the foliage (2) characteristic of the early part of the style, another is entirely without them, and approaches very closely to the Decorated (3).

The general appearance of Early English buildings is magnificent and rich, rather from the number of parts than from the details. In those buildings where very long windows are used there is a grandeur arising from the height of the divisions; in the smaller buildings there is much simplicity of appearance, but the work all appears well designed and carefully executed. It was usual to build the west front immediately after the choir, and leave the nave to be filled in afterwards.

Salisbury Cathedral is usually considered as THE TYPE of the Early English style, from the circumstance of its being less mixed than any other building of the same importance. It was commenced in 1220 on a new site, by Bishop Richard Poore, who died in 1237, and was buried in the choir, which was therefore completed at that time. The church was finished by Bishop Giles de Bridport, and consecrated in 1258.

The chapter-house at Christ Church, Oxford, the choir of Worcester Cathedral, a considerable part of Fountains Abbey, the choir of Rochester, the south transept of York, the presbytery of Ely, the nine altars of Durham at the east end, and the same part of Fountains Abbey, the choir of the Temple Church, London, and the nave of Lincoln, are well-known examples of this period, the first half of the thirteenth century.

In the year 1245, King Henry the Third, "being mindful of the devotion which he had towards St. Edward the Confessor, ordered the church of St. Peter at Westminster to be enlarged, and the eastern part of the walls, with the tower and transepts, being pulled down, he began to rebuild them in a more elegant style, having first collected at his own charges the most subtle artificers, both English and foreign." These portions of the church are the choir and apse; the work is of the richest character, but still pure Early English.

The north transept of York Minster was built between 1250 and 1260, by John the Roman, treasurer of the church, who afterwards became Archbishop of York. The records of this cathedral clearly prove that it was the regular practice of the chapter to keep a gang of workmen in their pay as part of the establishment; the number varied from twenty to fifty, and the same families were usually continued generation after generation: to their continued labour, always doing something every year, we are indebted for the whole of that glorious fabric. This practice was by no means peculiar to York, but appears to have been the usual custom.

This completes an outline of the Architectural history of the principal known buildings of the Early English style.

THE GRADUAL CHANGE FROM THE EARLY ENGLISH STYLE TO THE DECORATED.

THE change from the Early English to the Decorated style was so very gradual, that it is impossible to draw any line where one style ceases and the other begins. The time of Edward I. was that of the change, and some of our most beautiful examples belong to that period.

In the early Decorated the sculpture of the human figure is remarkable for the ease and chasteness of the attitudes, and the free and graceful, though at the same time rich, folds of the drapery. Few figures can surpass in simplicity and beauty the effigy of Queen Eleanor in Westminster Abbey, and those on the crosses erected to her memory are almost equally fine, especially those on the Northampton cross; those at Waltham have been mutilated and restored. They were all executed between 1291 and 1294, as appears by the builders' accounts, which are still extant. The cross at Geddington is perhaps the most perfect of those which remain. This is not mentioned in the executors' accounts, but probably only because that part of the accounts has been lost; it is as plainly a memorial cross to Queen Eleanor as either of the others.

Eleanor Cross, Geddington, A.D. 1295.   **Beverley, c. A.D. 1300.**

The three arches of the sedilia and the small one of the piscina at Harleston, Northants, may also be considered as transitional; the trefoil arch used under the pointed one, if taken by itself, would be Early English, and the moldings are deeply undercut, which is another mark of that style. On the other hand, the form of the moldings is that of a roll of parchment, and this form is more usually of the Decorated style.

The transepts of Westminster Abbey are recorded to have been built in his time, and they contain some of the most beautiful work that can be found anywhere; the capital next, with its natural foliage standing out quite free on the bell of the capital, would be considered as belonging to the Decorated style; but the deep undercutting of the abacus would rather belong to the Early English, and the roll-molding may be either Early English or Decorated. Some of the capitals are molded only, without foliage, and some of these have the abacus octagonal, which is more usual in French than in English work.

Some have proposed to divide the Decorated style into two—the geometrical and the flowing; but here the distinction is not sufficiently broad to constitute two distinct styles, although, as sub-divisions, these terms were used by Rickman himself, and are useful. But these two divisions are so frequently contemporaneous,

Sedilia and Piscina, Harleston Church, Northants, c. A.D. 1280.

and run into each other so continually, that it is almost impossible to separate them in practice: the windows may indeed be distinguished, though even in these we often find windows with geometrical tracery and others with flowing tracery in the same building, with the same moldings and details; and no distinction can be drawn in doorways and buttresses. It is better, therefore, to continue to use the received divisions of styles, and the received names for them. There is no broad line of distinction and of division in medieval buildings, it was one continual progress or decline; the divisions are arbitrary, but very convenient in practice.

The beautiful crosses erected by Edward I. at all the places where the body of Queen Eleanor had rested on its way from Grantham, Lincolnshire, where she died, to Westminster Abbey, where she was buried, all belong to this time of change, but are usually reckoned as early examples of the Decorated style. The accounts for preserving these are for the most part among the Public Records, but Geddington is not included, probably only because that account had been lost or mislaid in the Record Office, which was long much neglected; so much so, that for many years the valuable records were kept in the stables of Carlton House, the residence of the Prince Regent, afterwards George IV.

THE DECORATED STYLE. EDWARD I., II., AND III. A.D. 1272-1377.

Chancel, Stanton St. John, Oxon, c. A.D. 1320.

The choir of this church is an excellent example of the Decorated style, especially the east window. It is merely a parish church, not monastic.

THE name of the Edwardian style is sometimes given to this second Gothic style, which Rickman justly called DECORATED. The name of Edwardian implies the reigns of the three Edwards, and is convenient for England, but does not apply anywhere else, which is the objection to its general use.

THE PORCHES are sometimes shallow; others have a very bold projection, as at Kidlington; sometimes with windows or open arcades at the sides, and, though rarely, with a room over: there are also many fine timber porches of this style, distinguished by the moldings and barge-boards, as at Aldham, Essex. These wooden porches are common in some districts, as in Herefordshire, and rare in others. There are good examples at Binfield and Long Wittenham, Berkshire, although that is not one of the districts in which they are commonly met with.

There is frequently a niche over the outer doors, or door into the church from the porch; this was for the patron-saint. Occasionally, but rarely, there are remains of a wooden gallery in that position, supposed to have been for the choir-boys to stand when part of the marriage-ceremony was performed in the porch. There is frequently a staircase at the corner of the porch next the church, to ascend to the room over.

Kidlington, Oxon, c. A.D. 1350.

This porch is a good typical example of the outer doorway with the ball-flower ornament in the hollow molding, and the niche over it for the figure of the patron-saint.

Crick, Northants, c. A.D. 1320.

THE DOORWAYS of this style are frequently large, and very richly sculptured, and have a rich canopy over them, with crockets and finials, as at Crick, Northants; but in small churches they are as frequently plain, and have merely a dripstone over them, the roll-molding often terminated by two small heads, which are generally a king and a bishop; this is the case also with the windows. It is often not easy to distinguish the plain doorways of this style from those of the preceding one, but in general they are not so deeply

Dorchester, Oxon, c. A.D. 1320.

recessed. A few doorways of this style are double. When there are shafts in the jambs they are worked on the same stones, and not inserted as separate shafts of stone or marble, as in the Early English, and as at Dorchester, Oxon. The wooden doors are sometimes ornamented with panelling of a better description than that which is common in the next style; they were originally painted in colours like the interior of the churches, and often have ornamental iron-work upon them; even the nail-heads are made ornamental. This is also the case in the Early English style, and it is frequently not easy to distinguish one from the other, there being very little difference between them. In ordinary parish churches the old wooden door, with the original iron-work upon it, is often preserved longer than any other ornament.

East Window, North Aisle, Dorchester, Oxon, c. A.D. 1300.

THE DECORATED STYLE is distinguished by its large windows divided by mullions, and the tracery either in flowing lines, or forming circles, trefoils, and other geometrical figures, as at Dorchester, and not running perpendicularly; its ornaments are numerous and very delicately carved, more strictly faithful to nature and more essentially parts of the structure than in any other style. In small country churches, however, there are perhaps more very plain churches of this style than of any other; still the windows have the essential decoration of tracery. The ornament is also part of the construction, a point in which it differs from the other styles; a Decorated cusp cannot be inserted in the tracery.

Cloisters, Westminster Abbey, A.D. 1360.

There is a very fine window, with reticulated tracery and richly molded, in the south walk of the cloisters at Westminster. No rule whatever is followed in the form of the arch over windows in this style; some are very obtuse, others very acute, and the ogee arch is not uncommon. (See p. 141.)

Decorated tracery is usually divided into three general classes—geometrical, flowing, and flamboyant; the variety is so great, that many sub-divisions may be made, but they were all used simultaneously for a considerable period.

The earliest Decorated windows have geometrical tracery; Exeter Cathedral is, perhaps, on the whole, the best typical example of the early part of this style. The fabric rolls are preserved, and it is now evident that the existing windows are, for the most part, of the time of Bishop Quivil, from 1279 to 1291. The windows all have geometrical patterns, and some of these are identical with those of

Merton College Chapel, Oxford. The chancel of Haseley Church, Oxon, is a good example of the early Decorated style of Edward I. One of the windows in the cloisters of Westminster Abbey, p. 137, and the aisles of the choir of Dorchester Abbey Church, Oxon, p. 136, are also excellent examples.

The buildings of the time of Edward the First have geometrical tracery in the windows. In Merton College Chapel the side windows still retain the original painted glass, with the kneeling figure of the donor several times repeated, with the inscription "Magister Henricus de Mannesfeld," recorded by Wood as of A.D. 1283.

Many windows of this style, especially in the time of Edward I., have the rear-arch ornamented with cusps, with a hollow space over the head of the window in the thickness of the wall, between the rear arch and the outer arch.

Great Milton, Oxon, c. A.D. 1350.

Windows with flowing tracery, as at Great Milton, and in the church of the Austin Friars; also those with reticulated, or net-like forms, are in general somewhat later than the geometrical patterns; at least, they do not seem to have been introduced quite so early; but they are very frequently contemporaneous, and both classes may often be found side by side in the same building, evidently erected at the same time. An early instance of this occurs at Stoke Golding, in Leicestershire, built between 1275 and 1290, as appears by an inscription still remaining: the windows have mostly geometrical tracery, but several have flowing.

The Augustinian or Austin Friars, London, c. A.D. 1350.

The same mixture occurs at Selby Abbey, and St. Mary's, Beverley. In some instances windows with geometrical tracery have the moldings and the mullions covered with the ball-flower ornament in great profusion, even to excess: these examples occur chiefly in Herefordshire, as at Leominster; and in Gloucestershire, as in the south aisle of the nave of the Cathedral at Gloucester: they are for the most part, if not entirely, of the time of Edward II.

Finedon, c. A.D. 1350.   **Higham Ferrars, c. A.D. 1360.**

Finedon, and Higham Ferrars, Northants, are good examples of the ogee form of arch, and the manner in which the tracery is made to harmonise with the arch is very pleasing to the eye, and not very common.

What is called the net-like character of tracery, from its general resemblance to a fisherman's net, is very characteristic of this style at its best period, about the middle of the fourteenth century, of which there is a very fine example in the west window of the Franciscan Friary at Reading, p. 143, of which the remains are valuable, although a great deal of it was destroyed in the Georgian era, from the neglect that was usual at that period. It has been carefully restored in the time of Queen Victoria, at the expense of a gentleman of Reading, and is now used as a chapel-of-ease for the large parish in which it is situated. The roof now used at St. Mary's Church in Reading is said to have originally belonged to this chapel. One of the side windows, with a segmental head of the same period, is also a very good example of the style. This kind of tracery is the most usual characteristic of this style, and begins in the time of Edward II. There are good examples of this period in the south aisles of the churches of St. Mary Magdalene and St. Aldate's, Oxford.

The inner arch, or rear-arch, is frequently of a different shape and proportion to the outer one: there is also sometimes a series of open cusps hanging from it, called hanging foliation.

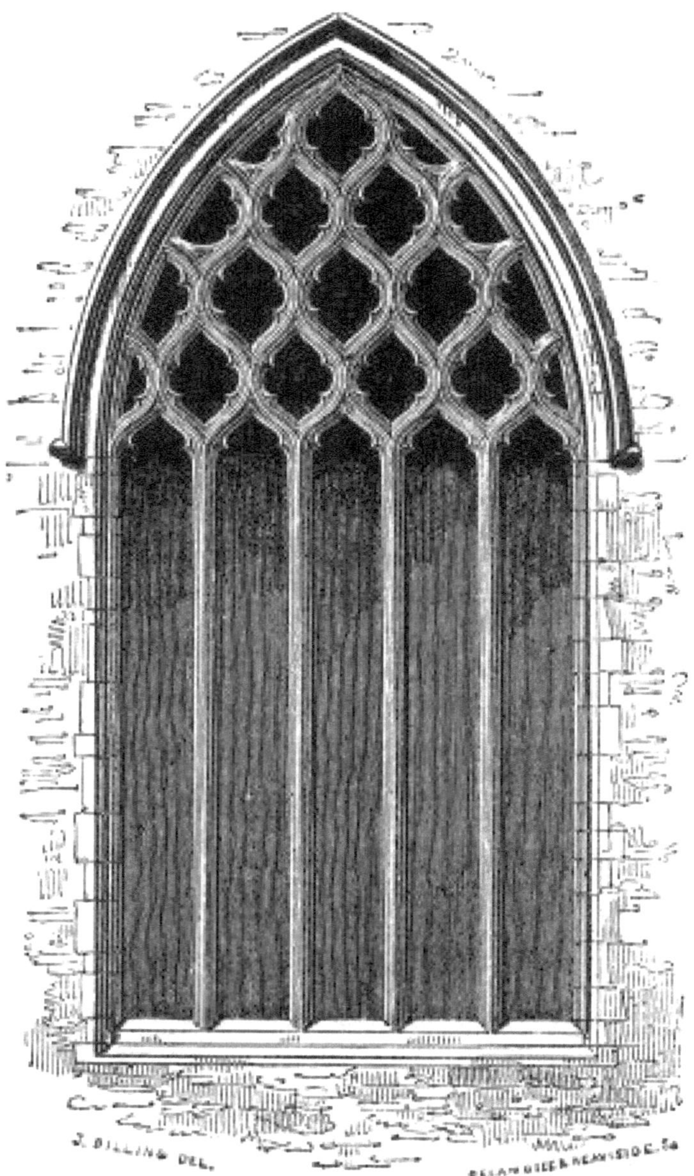

West Window, Franciscan Friary, Reading, c. A.D. 1350.

It is more common in some parts of the country than in others: this feature seems to have taken the place of the inner plane of decoration, with tracery and shafts, of the Early English style, and it disappears altogether in the succeeding style. There is a good example of this inner arch in Broughton Church, Oxfordshire. This foliated inner arch is not a very common feature.

Ardley, Oxon.

Square-headed windows are very common in this style in many parts of the country, especially in Leicestershire and in Oxfordshire, as at Ardley. Windows with a flat segmental arch are also frequently used in this style, and the dripstone, or projecting molding over the window to throw off the wet, is sometimes omitted, as at Stonesfield, which has also an elegant detached shaft in the interior.

Stonesfield, Oxon, North Window, c. A.D. 1320.
Interior and Exterior.

Windows in towers are usually different from those in other parts of the church. In the upper storey, where the bells are, there is no glass; in some parts of the country there is pierced stonework for keeping out the birds, but more usually they are of wood only. These are called sound-holes.

The storey under this, where the ringers stand, is also commonly called the belfry, and the windows of this storey are also peculiar, sometimes richly ornamented as at Irthlingborough, — where it is part of the work of Pyal, the founder of the college in that parish, A.D. 1388.

Clere-storey windows of this style are often small, and either circular with quatrefoil cusps, or trefoils or quatrefoils; or the spherical triangle with cusps, which forms an elegant window. The clever manner in which these windows are splayed within, and especially below, to throw down the light, should be noticed.

In some parts of the country, as in Oxfordshire, small clere-storey windows of the Decorated style, as at Great Milton and Garsington, are not uncommon, but more usually the churches have been rebuilt in the Perpendicular style, along with the roof, when the church has been raised.

DECORATED WINDOWS OF CLERE-STOREYS

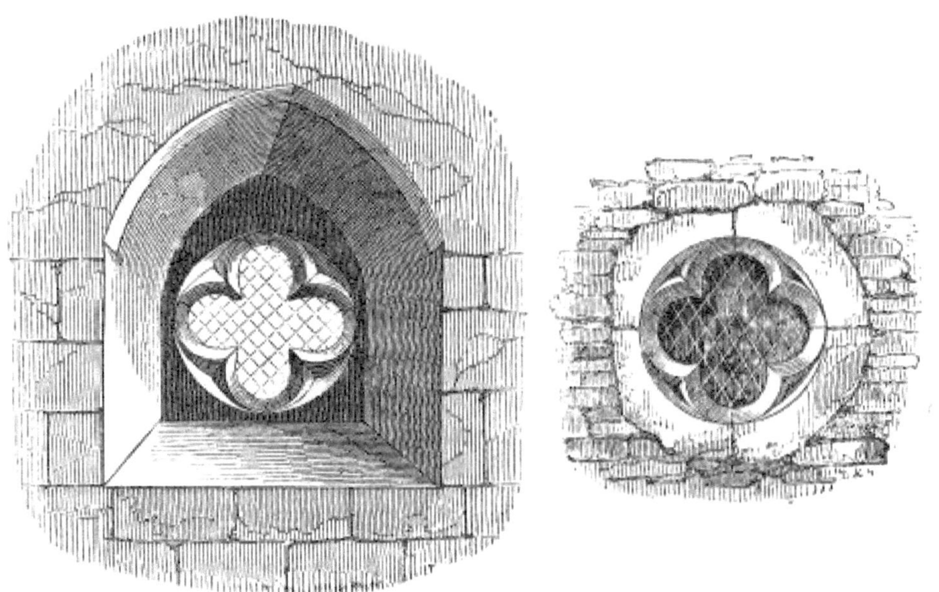

Interior.   **Exterior.**

Great Milton, Oxon, c. A.D. 1320.

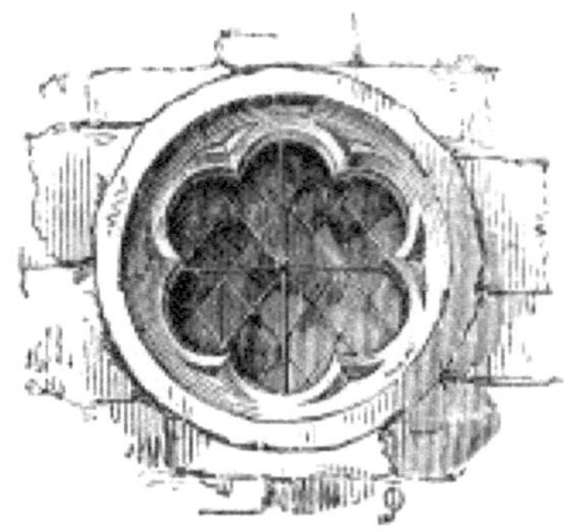

Garsington, Oxon, c. A.D. 1350.

Circular windows are also a fine feature of this style, chiefly used at the ends of the transepts in large churches, or at the west end in small ones. A rare instance of an east window of this form occurs at Westwell, Oxon, and a fine one on the side of a transept at Cheltenham.

Flamboyant tracery, and the forms approaching to it, generally indicate a late date. We have no instance of real Flamboyant work in this country, although forms of tracery approaching to it are not uncommon; the moldings are never of the true Flamboyant character, which is quite distinct both from the Decorated and the Perpendicular; it coincided in time with the latter, and therefore does not properly belong to our present subject.

The arch is sometimes cinquefoiled, and ornamented with crockets and bunches of foliage for finials, and with pinnacles also, as in Beverley Minster, where this arch is that of a canopy over a tomb, between two tall piers of a lofty arch. The ogee arch is frequently used in small arcades and in the heads of windows. The dripstones or hoodmolds are generally supported by heads, and are frequently enriched with crockets and finials. The most important are naturally those between the nave and aisles; those of the triforium, if there is one, as at Beverley, are not so tall, and are commonly divided into two in the same space as the one below.

DECORATED ARCHES.

Beverley, Yorkshire, c. A.D. 1350.

THE ARCHES do not differ very materially in general effect from the Early English, but are distinguished by the moldings and capitals as before described.

Beverley Minster, Yorkshire.

THE ARCADES which ornament the walls in rich buildings, and those over the sedilia, are very characteristic features of the style. In some instances the sedilia, or seats for the officiating clergy by the side of the altar, have projecting canopies over them, forming perfect tabernacles, as if for images; more commonly they have canopies on the same plane with the seats.

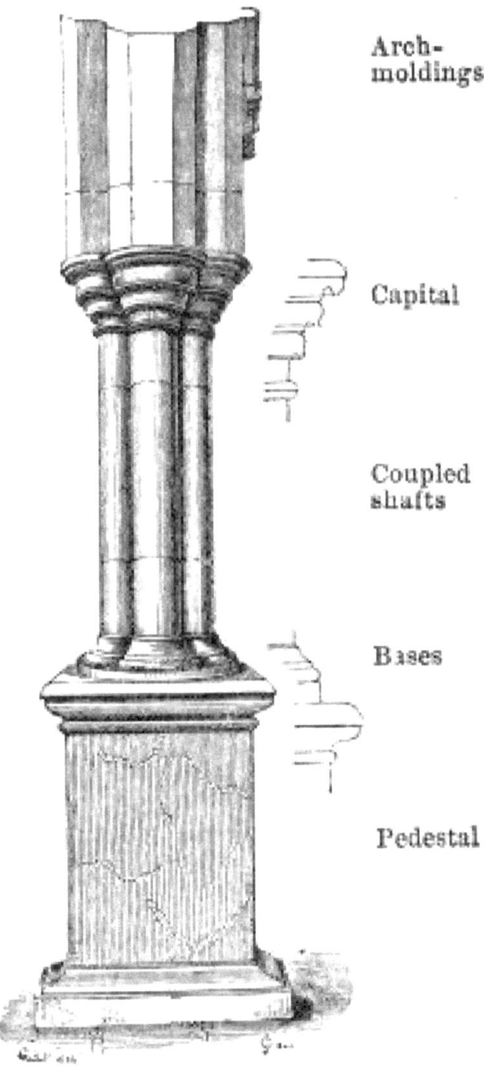

Naseby, Northants.

THE PILLARS have no longer detached shafts, and the capitals are ornamented with foliage of a different character from that which preceded it, as has been mentioned. Occasionally, though not very frequently, the base of the pillar is stilted upon a lofty plinth, as at Naseby, Northants. In a few instances, even in genuine work of the fourteenth century, this is done in a parish church merely for convenience, to raise the base above the level of the backs of the seats. This is an exceptional example, but is convenient as shewing beginners all the parts belonging to a pillar, the arch-molding resting upon the capital, and the pillar itself consisting of a cluster of shafts, with separate molded capitals and bases to the shafts that are united in one pillar, and the base resting upon a pediment.

In ordinary parish churches the pillars and arches are frequently as plain as in the Early English, and there is no very perceptible difference at first sight. In richer churches the pillars are clustered and the arches richly molded, and often have the hood-molding over them.

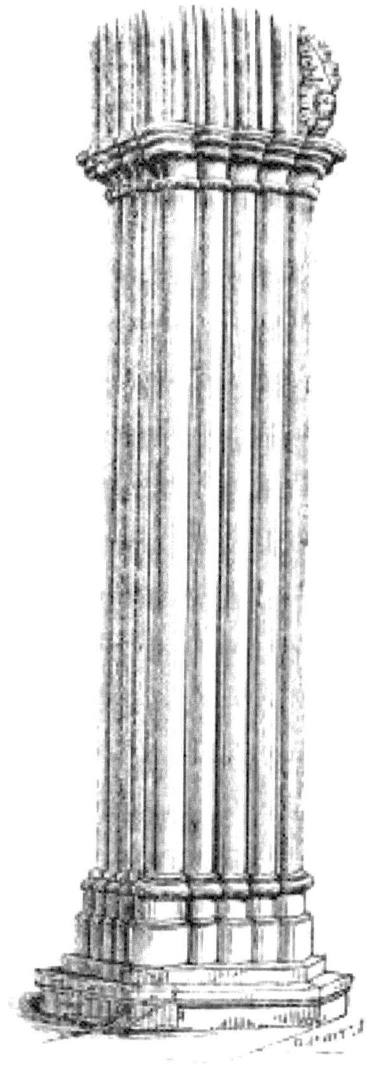

Exeter Cathedral, c. A.D. 1300.

The pillar is usually much more lofty than the one at Naseby (p. 151), and has in general a capital, or several smaller capitals, to the shafts that are united; there is not always any pediment, though there sometimes is, as at Frome, Somerset. More usually there is what is called a stilted base only. The example here given from Exeter Cathedral is an extremely good one of a clustered pillar, with molded capitals and stilted base. When there is foliage on the capital, it is usually longer, as in York Minster; but in this style, notwithstanding its name, the capitals are more frequently of moldings only, though the foliage obviously gives much more decoration.

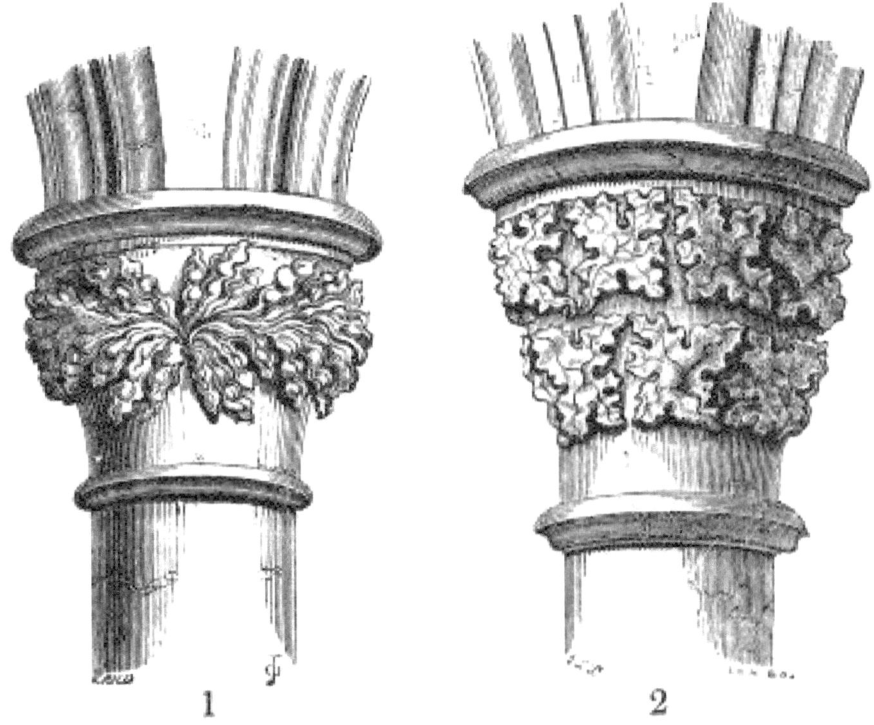

Beverley Minster, Yorkshire, c. A.D. 1320.

In the richer examples of this style, the CAPITALS are ornamented with beautiful foliage, each leaf being accurately copied from nature, as well as the best modern artist could do it. These were arranged so as to encircle the pillar, sometimes by means of a stalk forming a branch, as at Beverley (1). In other instances each leaf is separate, arranged round the bell of the capital, but by no means flat, and having almost as good an effect as when ranged upon stalks, as at Beverley (2). A large pier is sometimes a cluster of six shafts, each with its separate capital, some of which have foliage under a molded abacus, as at Beverley (3), others a series of moldings only. More frequently a pier consists of four shafts only, with a series of moldings for the capital, the upper or abacus being usually the roll-molding. Sometimes the hollows are rather deep, though not so deep as in the Early English, as at Beverley and Stanwick. In other instances there is no hollow, but the molding stands out clear from the bell of the capital, with a ring at the foot of it, as at

Irthlingborough.

The Bases are usually molded only, and stand upon a plinth, the height of which varies very much; it frequently happens that a new pavement of a church has raised the level several inches, which must, of course, be taken from the height of the base.

In small country churches, the pillars or piers are simply round or octagonal, and the arches that rest upon them are sometimes molded and sometimes not; but in richer churches the piers consist of a number of shafts clustered together, which add much to the effect. It frequently happens that four shafts are arranged diamond-wise, with a small hollow between them, as at Irthlingborough. There is sometimes a fillet on the shaft, or the shaft is pear-shaped; both of these occur in the same pillar at Beverley.

DECORATED CAPITALS.

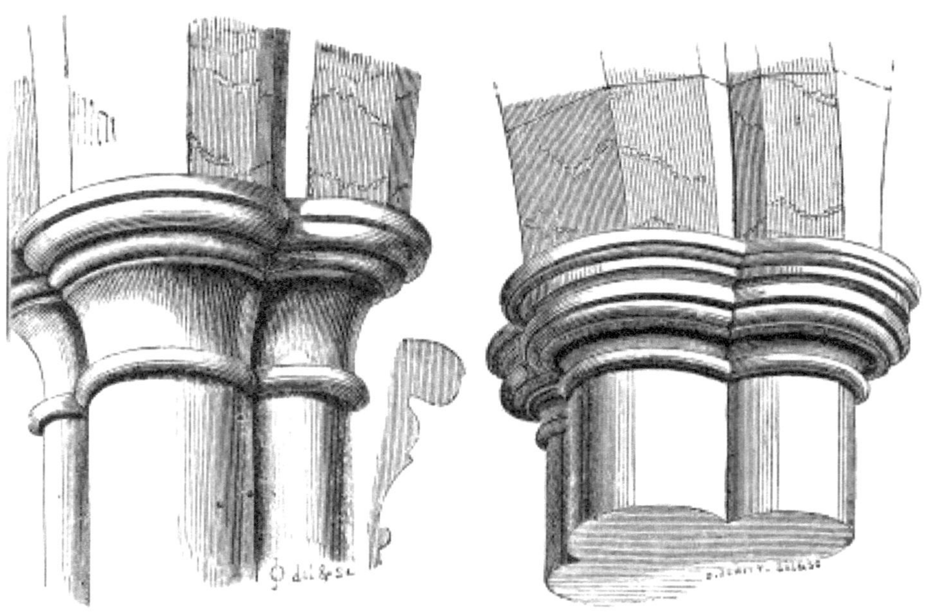

Irthlingborough, c. A.D. 1350.   Stanwick, c. A.D. 1320.

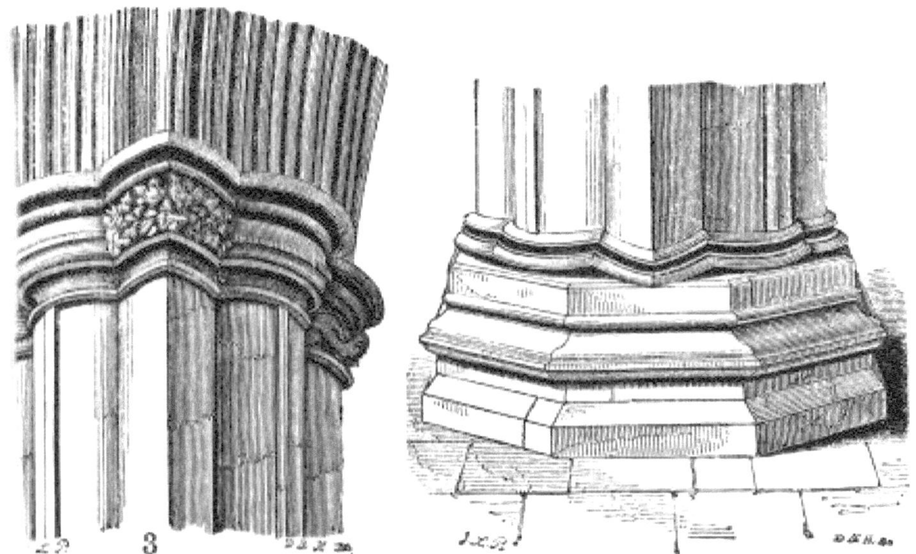

Capital and Base, Beverley, Yorkshire, c. A.D. 1320.

Sometimes there is a fillet on the edge, as at Beverley Minster (3); in other instances the edge is brought to a point, as in the same example. These clustered pillars add very much to the effect of the building; but this is not always noticed until they are drawn, and a section of them is shewn, and then the skill of the medieval architect has justice done to it. The moldings are chiefly shewn on the arches.

The roll-molding.

THE MOLDINGS of this style differ from the Early English chiefly in having the rounds and hollows not so deeply cut, and more generally filleted: the roll-molding, and the quarter round, are very much used; the abacus of the capital is in general a roll or filleted round, and the base is formed of round moldings without the deep hollow: as the style advances, the moldings become, generally, more shallow and feeble. The roll-molding is perhaps the most characteristic of the style, though it is used occasionally in Early English work also. A bold quarter-round is frequently used on arches without any other; the plain chamfer is used in all styles, but in Decorated work it is frequently sunk so as to leave a small square edge at each angle, thus varying the light and shade, and giving a precision to the angles of

DECORATED MOULDINGS.

Raunds, Northants, c. A.D. 1320.   Kidlington, Oxon, c. A.D. 1350.

Kidlington, Oxon, c. A.D. 1350.   Dorchester, Oxon, c. A.D. 1320.

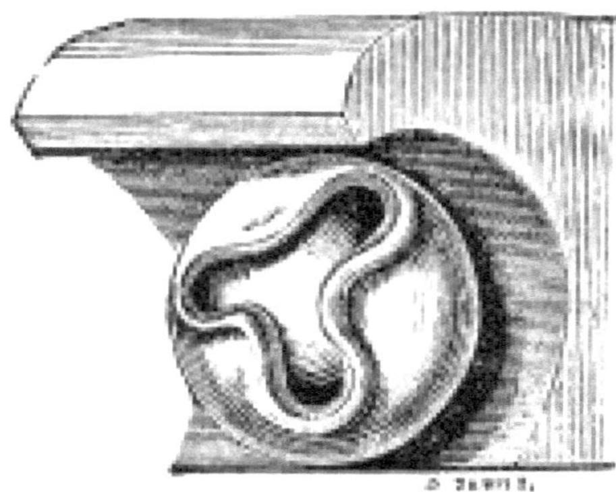

The ball-flower.

the chamfer which has a very good effect, as at Dorchester, p. 157. In late examples this is varied by a gentle swelling in the middle, forming a kind of shallow ogee molding, as at Kidlington. The ornamental sculptures in the hollow moldings are numerous, but there are two which require more particular notice; they are nearly as characteristic of the Decorated style as the zig-zag is of the Norman, or the tooth-ornament of the Early English. The first is the ball-flower, which is a globular flower half opened, and shewing, within, a small round ball. It is used with the utmost profusion in the moldings of windows, doorways, canopies, cornices, arches, &c., as at Raunds, Kidlington, and Dorchester (p. 157), generally with good effect, but sometimes in such excess as almost to destroy the effect of the moldings; but at the same time it gives great richness to the general effect of the windows. The ball-flowers are sometimes placed at intervals, and connected by a stem with or without foliage.

The other ornament is the four-leaved flower. This has a raised centre, and four petals cut in high relief; it is frequently much varied, but may be distinguished by its being cut distinctly into four petals, and by its boldness: it is sometimes used abundantly, though not quite so profusely as the ball-flower. In some instances the centre is sunk instead of being raised.

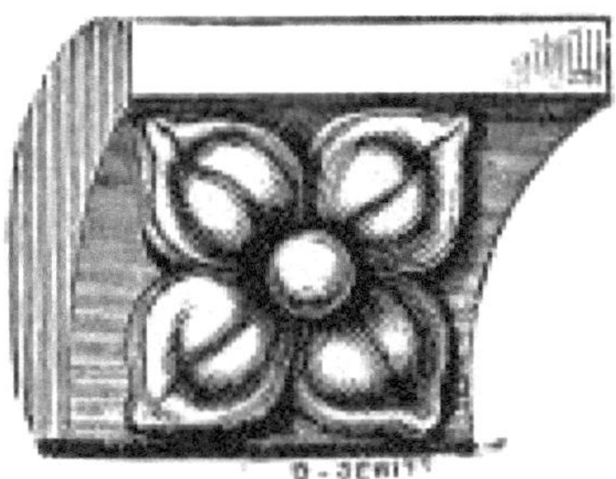

The four-leaved flower.

The battlement as an ornamental feature in the interior of buildings is frequently used in this style, although it is more common in the Perpendicular. Decorated battlements may generally be distinguished by the horizontal molding being cut off at each opening, and not continued vertically down the sides of it, as is usual in the later styles; and this applies to the actual battlement on the parapet, as well as to the merely ornamental battlement in the interior. It occurs on the top of a screen, or of a piscina or other niche; also on the transom, and sometimes on the sill of a window; in all which situations it is more common and more conspicuous in the Perpendicular style.

The use of the battlement as an ornament in the interior of a building, often on the edge of the sill of a window, is a singular caprice, but very common in English buildings; it is one of the English features that is much quizzed by the French architectural antiquaries.

The foliage in this style is more faithfully copied from nature than in any other: the vine-leaf, the maple, and the oak with the acorn, are the most usual. The surface of the wall is often covered with flat foliage, arranged in small squares called diaper-work, which is believed to have originated in an imitation of the rich hangings then in general use, and which bore the same name. These diaper patterns were originally coloured in imitation of the silks from which they were copied, and which at an early period came from the East, though they were afterwards imitated by the European manufacturers in Belgium and France, particularly at Ypres and Rheims. This kind of ornament was used in the Early English style, as in the choir of Westminster Abbey, but it more commonly belongs to the Decorated style. The colouring of the ornaments to make them more effective was far more common in mediæval Gothic work than is generally supposed, because it has been so universally whitewashed over, either by the Puritans, or during the bad taste of the Georgian era. This colouring frequently comes to light during modern restorations, when the whitewash is scraped off, and sometimes good pictures of scriptural subjects have been whitewashed over in the same ignorant manner.

Canterbury Cathedral, c. 1320.

Geddington Cross, Northamptonshire, c. 1295.

Buttresses of Chancel, Stanton St. John, Oxon.

THE BUTTRESSES in this style have great variety of forms and of degrees of richness. Sometimes they are quite plain, or merely have the angles chamfered off, and terminated by a slope, either under the cornice, as at Irthlingborough, or independent of it, as at Stanton St. John, Oxon. In other instances the buttress terminates in a pediment or gablet, as at Raunds, either with or without crockets and a finial, according to the richness of the building. Over each buttress there is frequently a gurgoyle, or ornamental water-spout. They usually have pediments, and are frequently enriched on the face with niches for figures (which sometimes, but rarely, are left), and canopies, and often terminate in pinnacles, as at Gadsby, Leicestershire. In large buildings there are fine arch-buttresses spanning over the aisles, as at Howden. There are sometimes also groups of pinnacles round the base of the spire in this style, which have a very rich effect, as at St. Mary's, Oxford.

DECORATED BUTTRESSES.

Irthlingborough, Northants, c. A.D. 1220.   **Raunds, Northants, A.D. 1250.**

These groups of pinnacles are among the most ornamental features of the style; those at the east end of Howden are among the most celebrated. The buttresses of this style are almost invariably divided into stages with a set-off between each, and sometimes have a succession of niches with crocketed canopies over them. Our eyes are so much accustomed to empty niches in this country that they do not offend us, but an empty niche is in fact an unmeaning thing, a niche was originally intended to contain an image, and the canopy over it was to protect the head of the image.

Howden, Yorkshire, c. A.D. 1350.

The flat surfaces in niches and monuments, on screens, and in other situations, are covered with delicately-carved patterns, called diaper-work, representing foliage and flowers; among which are introduced birds and insects, and sometimes dogs or other animals, all executed with much care and accuracy, and proving that the artists of that time drew largely from nature, the fountain-head of all perfection in art.

Sedilia, Chesterton, Oxon, c. 1320.

The sedilia, or seats for the officiating ministers on the east side of the altar, are frequently the most ornamental feature in the choir of a parish church; as at Chesterton, Oxon, in which they are very elegant, with light shafts and the ball-flower molding. These, with the piscinas, are frequently the only ornamental features in a country church, which is in other respects quite plain; the name Decorated is sometimes objected to on this ground, but the name has special reference to the window-tracery, which in the Decorated is a necessary part of the construction; this is not the case in the Early English style.

THE PISCINAS, or water-drains, and niches, or tabernacles for images, are often very rich, with canopies and open tracery. These objects commonly shew the chief beauties of this style; they are always on the south side of the altar, the locker or ambry for keeping the chalice, &c., is usually on the north side. The pediment, or straight-sided canopy, is much used in this style over doors, sedilia, piscinas, and monuments.

The Groined Roofs, or Vaults, are distinguished from those of the preceding style chiefly by an additional number of ribs, and by the natural foliage on the bosses. Many fine examples of these remain, as in the Cathedral of Exeter, and at York in the chapter-house; at Norwich in the cloisters; at Chester[5] the vault is of wood, with stone springers. There are a few instances of stone roofs of this style over narrow spaces of very high pitch, supported by open-work, as if in imitation of wood-work, as on the vestry of Willingham, Cambridgeshire, and the porch of Middleton Cheney, Oxfordshire.

DECORATED PISCINAS.

Rushden, Northants, c. A.D. 1350.

Enford, Wilts, c. A.D. 1350.

---

[5] The wooden groined vaults of Chester Cathedral were carefully restored in 1871-72, with excellent effect, and in very good taste.

Ambry, or Locker, with the Door,   **Piscina, Tackley, Oxon.**

Rushden, Northants, c. A.D. 1350.

TIMBER ROOFS of this period are comparatively scarce, although they are more common than is usually supposed; but it is lamentable to observe how fast they are disappearing: that of the hall of the abbey of Great Malvern, the finest example that existed in this country, or probably in any other, was wantonly destroyed: it was a wooden ceiling, with an outer roof.

Bradenstoke Priory, or Clack Abbey, near Chippenham, in Wiltshire, is, or was, a fine example. The timber roofs of churches of this style are not generally so fine as those of halls. There are, however, many very good specimens of Decorated roofs remaining in churches, as at Adderbury, Oxfordshire, Raunds, Northamptonshire, and several others in that neighbourhood.

It should be observed that what are called open timber roofs are, very frequently, inner roofs or ceilings for ornament only, with a plain substantial outer roof over them, as at Sparsholt, Berkshire. These inner roofs or wooden ceilings, are sometimes of precisely the same form as stone vaults, which are, in fact, ceilings of another kind. The wooden vaults of Warmington and the cloisters of Lincoln have been already mentioned; those of the nave of York Minster and Winchester Cathedral are also of wood only. At Kiddington, Oxfordshire, is a good example of a Decorated timber-roof of an ordinary parish church. At Kidlington, in the same county, there is also a Decorated timber-roof to the south aisle of the nave.

Kiddington, Oxon, c. A.D. 1350.

Ceilings are very useful and often necessary, and the proper thing to be considered is how best to make them ornamental also, as they were formerly. The Puritan fashion of plain whitewashed plaster ceilings caused a natural prejudice against ceilings altogether, which has been carried too far. These were introduced in the seventeenth century, and continued during the ignorant and apathetic eighteenth, and first half of the nineteenth. In some instances these flat plaster ceilings entirely concealed the upper part of fine Decorated windows; this was notably the case in the fine church of Haseley, Oxfordshire; the plaster ceiling had there been introduced in the time of George the Third. This church was the first to be restored by the Oxford Architectural Society, and the first in which open-seats were restored in the diocese of Oxford.

The open timber-roofs of the Victorian Gothic architects, whether in what are miscalled *restorations* or in new churches, have quite a distinct character of their own, a general imitation of the time of Edward the First or Second; but no one with eyes in his head can mistake *these* for old work, although in some of the *real* restorations the work is so well done that inexperienced eyes are frequently deceived. In roofs and painted glass this is never the case; the English painted glass of the Decorated style is generally very good, with grey backgrounds, and bands of figures in colour, which are thus well seen; in modern glass, bright colours are put in the backgrounds, and destroy the effect of the figures. The roofs are also generally a bad imitation of the old work.

Moulton, Northants.

THE TOWERS of the Decorated style are usually placed at the west end, and follow very much the same general appearance as in the Early English, but of course with the doorways, and windows, and other features characteristic of the style. The cornice is also generally richer, with a panelled battlement, and with gargoyles projecting from it at the corners, and pinnacles at the angles, as at Moulton, Northants, where the lower part of the pinnacles only remain. Sometimes there appears to have been a wooden spire, but this is by no means always the case.

Wollaston, Northants, c. A.D. 1310.   Ringstead, Northants, c. A.D. 1350.

THE SPIRES of the Decorated style differ but slightly from those of the Early English, excepting that there are generally more of the spire-lights, small windows at the bases and on the sides of the spire, as at Wollaston and Ringstead, Northants.

THE EAST FRONT of a church of this style most commonly consists of one large window at the end of the choir, flanked by tall buttresses, and a smaller one at the end of each aisle; the west front usually has the same arrangement, with the addition of a doorway, or doorways, under the central window, but there are frequently two narrow windows, with a buttress between them carrying a bell-cot, in small country churches of this style. The east ends of Carlisle and Selby, and the west end of Howden, are among the finest examples. On the Continent the large rose-window is almost always a principal feature of the west front; with us it is comparatively rare, and more often found in the transept ends than at the west end. The south fronts of Howden and Selby are also fine examples of the arrangement of the side of a large building of this style, with large windows both to the aisle and the clere-storey, separated by buttresses with pinnacles. The interior of the choir at Selby is one of the finest examples of the general effect of a Decorated interior, and on a smaller scale the choirs of Hull, and of Dorchester, Oxfordshire, are good examples. Lichfield Cathedral has the great advantage of having its three spires perfect, and on this account perhaps gives us the best idea of the effect intended to be produced by the exterior of a perfect church of this style: there can be no doubt that the same arrangement was contemplated in many other instances.

The lantern of Ely and the nave of York must not be omitted in this mention of some of the leading examples of the Decorated style, the general character of which is thus ably summed up by MR. RICKMAN:—

"THE GENERAL APPEARANCE of Decorated buildings is at once simple and magnificent; simple from the small number of parts, and magnificent from the size of the windows, and the easy flow of the lines of tracery. In the interior of large buildings we find great breadth, and an enlargement of the clere-story windows, with a corresponding diminution of the triforium, which is now rather a part of the clere-storey opening than a distinct member of the division. The roofing, from the increased richness of the groining, becomes an object of more attention. On the whole, the nave of York, from the uncommon grandeur and simplicity of the design, is certainly the finest example; ornament is nowhere spared, yet there is a simplicity which is peculiarly pleasing."

THE GRADUAL CHANGE FROM DECORATED TO PERPENDICULAR. RICHARD II. AND THE LATTER PART OF EDWARD III. FROM C. 1360 TO 1399.

Having now traced the gradual development of Gothic architecture, from the rudest Romanesque to its perfection in the Decorated style, it only remains to trace its decline, which, though not equally gradual, was much more so than is commonly supposed. Up to the time of its perfection the progress appears to have been nearly simultaneous throughout the northern part of Europe, with some exceptions; but during the period of its decline, chiefly the fifteenth and sixteenth centuries, it assumed a different form in each country, so distinct one from the other as to require a different name, and to be fairly considered as a distinct style. To call the Perpendicular style of England by the same name as the Flamboyant style of France, Germany, and the Low Countries, can only cause needless confusion; and the received names for these styles are so expressive of their general character that it would not be easy to improve upon them.

The gradual change from the Decorated to the Perpendicular style has been less generally noticed than the earlier transitions; but though less apparent at first sight, it may be as clearly traced, and examples of it are almost equally numerous: they occur in most parts of the country, though more common in some districts than in others, especially in Norfolk.

Professor Willis has demonstrated that this change began to shew itself, in the choir and transepts of Gloucester Cathedral, before the middle of the fourteenth century. The panelling and the window tracery have so much the appearance of the Perpendicular style that they have been commonly supposed to have been rebuilt or altered at a late period; but the vaulting and the moldings are pure Decorated, and the painted glass of the fourteenth century is evidently made for the places which it occupies in the heads of the windows with Perpendicular tracery: it must therefore be considered as the earliest known example of this great change of style. In this work of alteration the walls and arches of the Norman church were not rebuilt, but cased with panelling over the inner surface, so as to give the effect of the latter style to the interior. This was just the same process as was afterwards followed at Winchester by William of Wykeham, in changing the Norman to the Perpendicular style in appearance without any actual rebuilding. The work was begun as early as 1337, and carried on for a number of years. The funds were procured by offerings at the tomb of King Edward II., who, as is well known, was buried in this church, the body having been removed from Berkeley Castle for that purpose by the Abbot Thokey. It has been ascertained by Archdeacon Freeman, at Exeter, by a careful comparison of the building with the fabric rolls, that the greater part of that fine Cathedral was also *altered* from the Norman to the Decorated style without rebuilding.

The Dean's Cloister of Windsor with the buildings surrounding it was built between 1350 and 1356, as appears by the builder's accounts still extant in the Public Record Office. The style is Perpendicular, but with Decorated moldings, or at least a mixture of them. The vault of the porch under the Ærary or treasury, and the doorway to it, are among the richest pieces of work of this period. It was originally the porch of the chapter-house of the Order of the Garter.

Sir G. G. Scott, in his "Gleanings from Westminster Abbey," has also shewn that part of the cloisters, and some other work recorded to have been built by Abbot Litlington, 1362-1386, are in a style of transition, belonging rather to the Perpendicular than the Decorated.

Window of the Hall of the Abbot's House, now the Scholars' Hall, Westminster, A.D. 1376-1386.

The substructure of all the canonical residences running southward from the Deanery, (itself the Abbot's house of old,) displays a range of vaulting of simple and elegant character, with here and there a window of the period still remaining to testify that the whole was completed, before the tasteless alterations of subsequent centuries destroyed the workmanship which they were as unable to appreciate as to imitate. Two archways still remain, in the length of this substructure, connecting Great Dean's Yard with the courts to the eastward of it. They are of the style to which their known date would assign them; though perhaps a close consideration of their details (such as the cavetto and double ogee moldings) would lead to the conclusion that those characteristics, hitherto assigned to the fifteenth century, are here found in one of the earliest examples of their application.

The whole of Abbot Litlington's work is in a style of transition between the Decorated and Perpendicular period; it is almost impossible to say to which of these received styles the moldings and details can be referred. As the divisions of the styles of Gothic Architecture are entirely arbitrary, arranged for general convenience, and for the use of beginners in the study, it is perfectly natural that this sort of mixture should take place for a certain period between each of the great changes. The latter part of the fourteenth century was the period when the Perpendicular style was coming into general use, but was not fully established: as the distinction is less marked than in the similar period between each of the other styles, it has been commonly overlooked, but the same overlapping of styles occurs at this period as in the similar transition between the others. This is more marked and prominent between the Norman and the Early English styles, and therefore that is commonly called *the* period of transition; but a similar period exists equally between each, a gradual change was always going on.

Part of the Vaulting of the Cloisters over the Lavatory, Abbot Litlington's Work,

Westminster Abbey, A.D. 1376-1386.

One of the earliest authenticated examples of this transition is the church of Edington, Wiltshire, built by William de Edington, Bishop of Winchester: the first stone was laid in 1352, and the church was dedicated in 1361. It is a fine cruciform church, all of uniform character, and that character is neither Decorated nor Perpendicular, but a very remarkable mixture of the two styles throughout. The tracery of the windows looks at first sight like Decorated, but on looking more closely the introduction of Perpendicular features is very evident. The west doorway has the segmental arch common in Decorated work; over this is the usual square label of the Perpendicular, and under the arch is Perpendicular panelling over the heads of the two doors: the same curious mixture is observable in the moldings, and in all the details. This example is the more valuable from the circumstance that it was Bishop Edington who commenced the alteration of Winchester Cathedral into the Perpendicular style; he died in 1366, and the work was continued by William of Wykeham, who mentions in his will that Edington had finished the west end, with two windows on the north side and one on the south: the change in the character of the work is very distinctly marked. Bishop Edington's work at Winchester was executed at a later period than that at Edington, and, as might be expected, the new idea is more fully developed; but on a comparison between the west window of Winchester and the east window of Edington, it will at once be seen that the principle of construction is the same; there is a central division carried up to the head of the window, and sub-arches springing from it on each side: it may be observed that whenever this arrangement of the sub-arches occurs in Decorated work, it is a sign that the work is late in the style. Before the death of Bishop Edington the great principles of the Perpendicular style were fully established. Those chiefly consist of the Perpendicular lines through the head of the window, and in covering the surface of the wall with panelling of the same kind. These features are as distinctly marked at Winchester as in any subsequent building, or as they well could be.

The next great work of Wykeham was New College Chapel, Oxford, certainly one of the earliest, perhaps the first, building erected from the foundations entirely in the Perpendicular style; and a finer specimen of the style does not exist. The first stone was laid in 1380, and it was dedicated in 1386. Winchester College, built immediately after New College, is of precisely the same character with it, as might have been expected: they are both excellent specimens for the study of the Perpendicular style. Another very remarkable and valuable example of the transition from Decorated to Perpendicular is the choir of York Minster, commenced by Archbishop John de Thoresby in 1361, and completed in 1408; the general appearance of this magnificent work is Perpendicular, but there is great mixture in all the details. The chancel of St. Mary's Church at Warwick, rebuilt by Thomas Beauchamp, second Earl of Warwick, between 1370 and 1391, has more of the Perpendicular, being covered with panelling like Winchester, but the moldings are quite of mixed character. King's Sutton Church, Northamptonshire, deserves notice as a specimen of this transition. In some instances, as at Charlton-on-Otmoor, the perpendicular line of the molding is carried on straight through the flowing lines of the tracery to the arch.

East Window, Charlton-on-Otmoor, Oxon, c. 1380.

The nave and western transepts of Canterbury Cathedral were rebuilt between 1378 and 1411, but the Perpendicular style was then so fully established that there are scarcely any signs of transition. Chipping-Camden Church, Gloucestershire, was rebuilt by William Greville, a rich wool-stapler, who is buried in the chancel with his wife, and there is a fine brass to their memory; he died in 1401. This church is almost entirely of transitional character. The glorious chapter-house of Howden, and Gisburne Priory Church, in Yorkshire, are of this period, and very fine examples of early Perpendicular work. The roof and the casing of the walls of Westminster Hall belong also to the close of this century, 1397-99. The gatehouse of Thornton Abbey, Lincolnshire, is another splendid example of this transition. The cloisters of Gloucester Cathedral are decided Perpendicular in the fan-tracery of the vaults, but are partly of earlier date and character.

Houses and castles of the time of Richard II. are rather numerous and fine, and have frequently such a mixture of the Decorated and Perpendicular styles that it is difficult to say to which they belong. This is the case with a part of Warwick Castle, of Donnington Castle, Berkshire, Wardour Castle, Wiltshire, and Wressel Castle, Yorkshire; and Bolton Castle, in the more northern part of Yorkshire, is another fine example, and remarkably perfect. It is a very lofty and fine building, rather a fortified house than a castle intended for military purposes; there are two courts, and all the towers are perfect, or nearly so. It belongs to the time of Richard II. Dartington Hall, Devonshire, near Totnes, is another remarkable example of this period and character; it is a manor-house not fortified, with extensive farm-buildings attached to it. All the original windows are of four lights, with arches of the form called the shouldered-arch, which has been adopted in the modern Gothic front of Balliol College, Oxford. The original parts of the Vicar's Close at Wells are of the same character and period; the remains of the Vicar's Close at Lincoln are in part also of this character, one house is earlier, more decidedly Edwardian, and remarkably perfect. Most of these buildings are well known and have often been described, but are sometimes said to belong to the one style and sometimes to the other, this important transitional period having been very commonly overlooked.

The chancel of the fine church at Warwick is an excellent example of this change; it has sometimes been described as of the earlier style, and by other writers as of the later. The chapel on the south side of it, with the celebrated tomb of the Earl of Warwick, is an addition, and belongs to the later style.

THE PERPENDICULAR STYLE. RICHARD II. TO HENRY VIII. A.D. 1377-1547.

HAVING thus taken a rapid historical survey of the introduction of the Perpendicular style, it should be mentioned that this style is exclusively English, *it is never found* on the Continent, and it has the advantage of being more *economical* in execution than the earlier styles. It remains to describe its characteristic features. The broad distinction of the Perpendicular style lies in the form of the tracery in the head of the windows; and in fully developed examples the distinction is sufficiently obvious. We have no longer the head of the window filled with the gracefully flowing lines of the Decorated tracery, but their place is supplied by the rigid lines of the mullions, which are carried through to the architrave moldings, the spaces between being frequently divided and subdivided by similar Perpendicular lines; so that *Perpendicularity* is so clearly the characteristic of these windows, that no other word could have been found which would at once so well express the predominating feature. The same character prevails throughout the buildings of this period: the whole surface of a building, including its buttresses, parapets, basements, and every part of the flat surface, is frequently covered with panelling, in which the Perpendicular line clearly predominates; and to such an excess is this carried that the windows frequently appear to be only openings in the panel-work. This is equally apparent at the beginning, in the interior of the west end of Winchester Cathedral, and in the exterior of the Divinity School, Oxford, near the end of this style. The towers of Boston in Lincolnshire, and Evesham in Worcestershire, are also fine examples of exterior panelling. Panelling, indeed, now forms an important feature of the style; for though it was used in the earlier styles, it was not to the same extent, and was of very different character, the plain surfaces in those styles being relieved chiefly by diaper-work.

Fotheringhay, Northants, A.D. 1435.

A remarkable example of a Perpendicular church, the contract for build-ing which has been preserved, and was published by Mr. Hartshorne for the Oxford Architectural Society in 1841.

In the earlier or transitional examples we find, as has been mentioned, a mix-ture of the two styles. The general form of the tracery is frequently Decorated, but the lines of the mullions are carried through them, and perpendicular lines in various ways introduced. A very common form of transition is the changing of the flowing lines of a two-light Decorated window into a straight-sided figure by the introduction of perpendicular lines from the points of the sub-arches, as at Haseley, Oxfordshire. Sometimes we have Decorated moldings, with Perpendic-ular tracery, but frequently the features of both styles are intimately blended, and produce a very good effect.

This peculiarly English style is found far more convenient for domestic build-ings than the earlier styles. There are a large number of palaces and houses of this style remaining, such as nearly all the colleges of Oxford and Cambridge; it can also be very well executed in brickwork. Some of the finest mediæval houses that we have remaining are of brick, and the tall brick chimneys of this style are both ornamental and convenient; they are usually built in the outer wall, and carried up above the level of the roof, and for this reason the fires made under such chimneys never smoke. Modern builders have greatly neglected this precaution, and the wind blowing over a high-pitched roof naturally descends on the other side, and carries the smoke down the chimney, instead of letting it float away freely with the wind.

No one who has seen the fine brick buildings of the time of Henry the Seventh can despise them. Eton College is almost entirely built of brick, excepting the chapel, which is faced with stone. In many districts the difference of expense between brick and stone is enormous. The old Romans were quite aware of this, and used brick far more than modern builders are willing to do, even for their imperial palaces and magnificent aqueducts.

The arches of this style are not usually so acute as in the earlier periods, and in the latter part of the style become very flat, but in the earlier portion they are similar to the previous style, as in the compartment of Fotheringhay. In this instance there is also a deep hollow molding, which looks at first sight like Decorated, and beginners in the study are frequently misled by this feature, but it is often continued for the first half of the Perpendicular period. The arch of the clere-storey window over the former is comparatively flat. The name of *clere-storey* is usually continued even when there is no *triforium*, or blind-storey, as it is called by William of Worcester, writing in the fifteenth century. The French have adopted the English name of *clear-storey*, with the old spelling [as clèrestorie]: it is therefore more expedient to observe it, but for beginners it may perhaps be necessary to explain that *clere* is the old spelling of 'clear.' The different forms of the two arches of the windows of the aisle and of the clere-storey in this dated example, prove that the form of the arch is never a safe guide to the date of a building; to fix a date, various details have often to be considered.

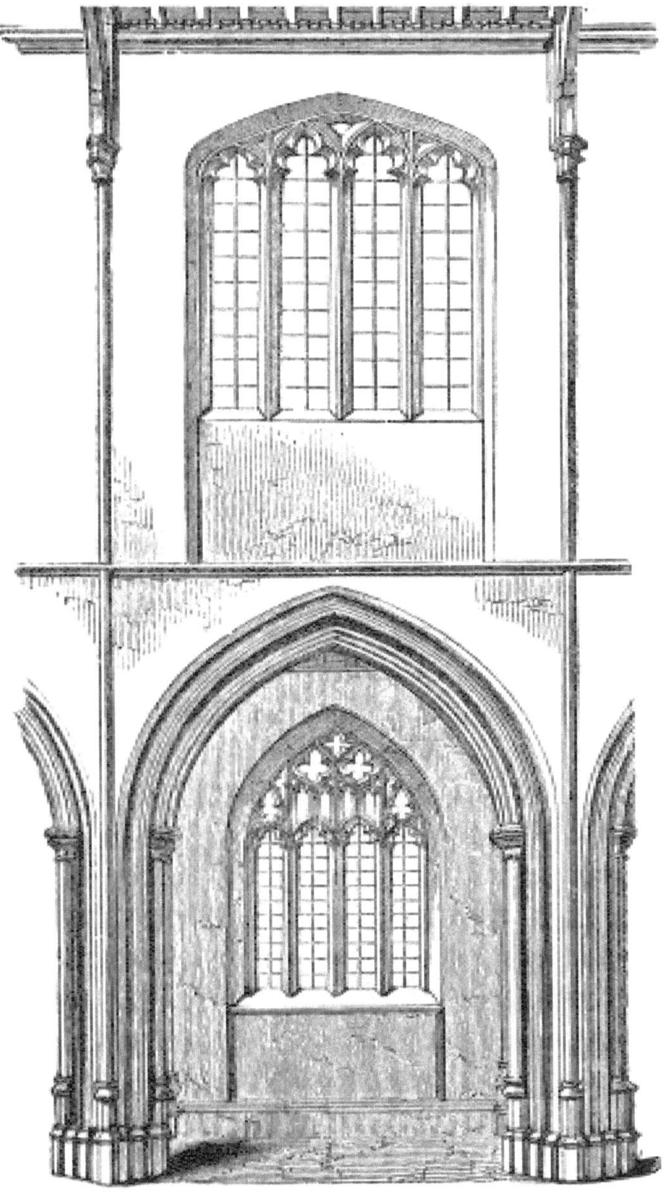

Compartment of Fotheringhay Church, A.D. 1435.

Waterperry, Oxon.

Arch over a tomb of a knight in plate armour, of the fifteenth century.

It is not always easy to distinguish at first sight the arch over a tomb of early Perpendicular from one in the Decorated style, as at Waterperry, Oxon. Here the battlement on the top of the wall at the back, and the plate-armour of the knight, and the crockets on the ogee arch, are more like the Decorated style.

The capitals and bases of columns in this style can generally be distinguished by the shallowness of the moldings, sometimes panelling is introduced; one of this kind, with the base stilted and molded, is in the Lady-chapel at Winchester. Foliage, if used, is generally shallow, and not so good as in the Decorated.

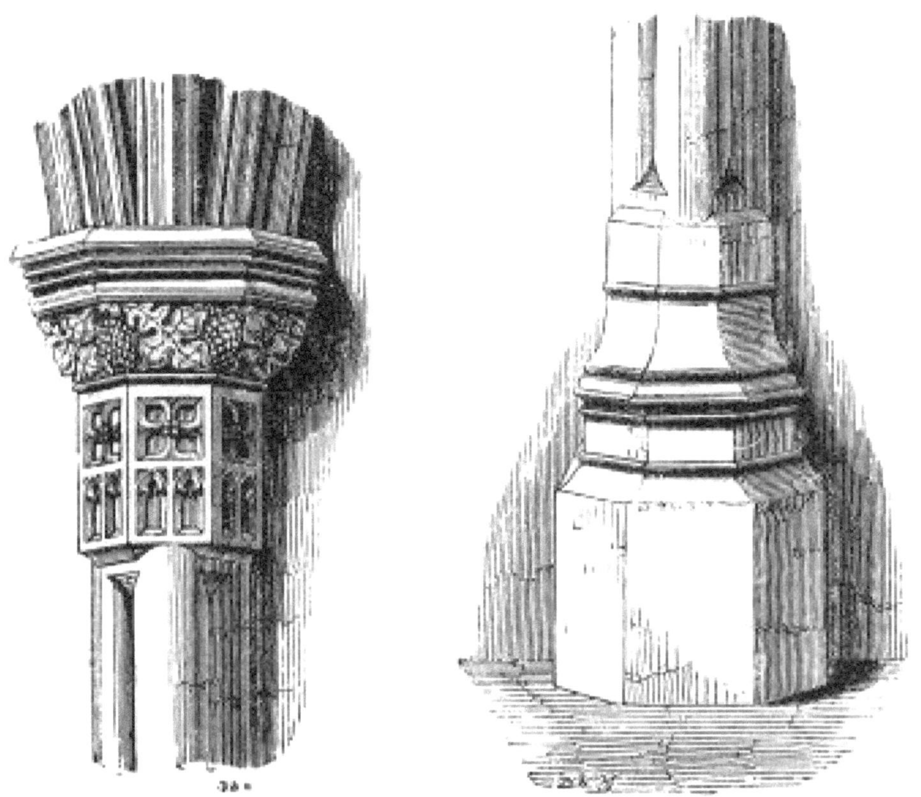

Lady-chapel, Winchester, c. A.D. 1460.

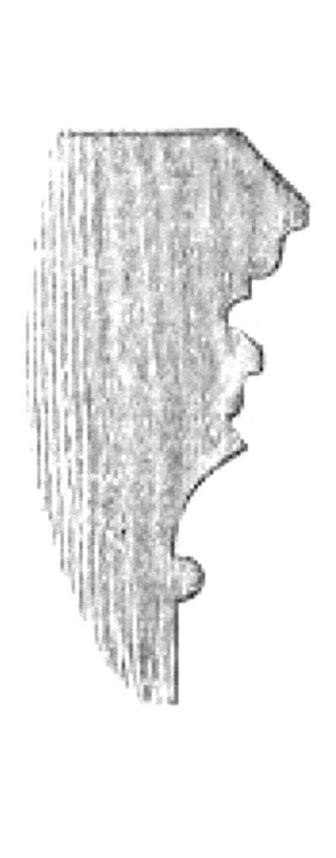

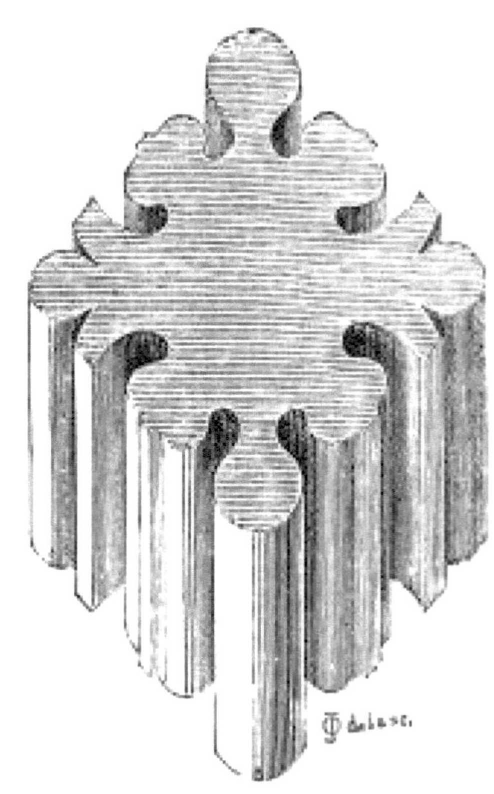

Section of the Capital of Pier.   Pier, Fotheringhay, A.D. 1435.

The columns themselves are frequently so much like those of the Decorated style, especially in plain parish churches, that they can hardly be distinguished excepting by the moldings on the capitals and bases, if there are any, but there are no bases in many instances. At Fotheringhay, which is a particularly valuable example as having a given date for all parts of it, the columns, pillars, or piers, for they are called by all three names, have a great resemblance to the Decorated style.

THE WINDOWS of New College and the ante-chapel of Merton College, Oxford, afford perhaps as fine examples as are to be found of early and perfect Perpendicular. They are both what is called sub-arcuated, but in New College the window is of four lights, and the sub-arches rise from the centre mullion; while in Merton, which is of three lights, the mullions are carried up to the architrave, and the side lights only are sub-arcuated. Both these forms are very frequent. In many later examples these sub-arches are entirely disused, and all the mullions are carried through the transom; this is the case at New College; but it was afterwards used to excess, so as greatly to injure the effect of the windows.

William of Wykeham, New College, Oxford, A.D. 1386.

Shewing Perpendicular tracery, with sub-arches and a transom, the heads of the
lights cinquefoiled (five foiled).

Haseley, Oxon, c. A.D. 1480.

In the later examples the arches of the windows are much lower than they were in the earlier period, and the four-centred arch, which began now to be extensively used, was gradually depressed, until all beauty of proportion was lost, the arches being little more than two straight lines rounded at the angle of junction with the jambs. These late windows had frequently great width in proportion to their height, as at Haseley, and were placed so near together, that the strength of the building entirely depended on the buttresses.

Presbytery, York, c. A.D. 1460.

A little later in the style, one of the best examples that is anywhere to be found is the Presbytery at York, in which the windows are very large and divided into five lights; in the central division the mullions are carried straight through the arch, and two horizontal transoms are introduced, which is a very unusual arrangement; there are also transoms across the side lights on each side, and there are two of them.

These windows having all been originally filled with painted glass, we have rarely an opportunity of judging of the proper effect of them; the glare of light which we now complain of having been caused by the destruction of that material, which was intended to soften and partially to exclude it. The church of Fairford, in Gloucestershire, affords a rare instance of the painted glass having been preserved in all the windows, and the effect is solemn and calm—very far from glaring; and it is remarkable that they impede the light so little that a book may be read in any part of the church, which is seldom the case with modern painted glass. The clere-storeys also are frequently almost a sheet of glass merely divided by lighter or heavier mullions, thus offering a complete contrast to the small and distant openings so frequently found in Early English and Decorated work. Square-headed, segmental, and other flat-arched windows, are frequent in this style. In rich churches there is sometimes a double plane of tracery, the one glazed, the other not. In the choir of York the inner one is glazed. The east window of the nave of Chipping-Norton Church, Oxfordshire, over the chancel-arch, is a fine specimen of this kind of window: in this instance the outer plane is glazed.

THE DOORWAYS are frequently very rich, but have generally one prevailing form, which is a depressed arch within a square frame, and over this a label.

S. Crux, York, c. A.D. 1420.

Fine examples of panelled wooden doors of this style are also met with occasionally, as in the church of S. Crux, at York. The priest's door, on the south side of the chancel, is often an insertion of a later period than the building, and is of this style, although the walls may be Early English or Decorated.

The label-molding is frequently filled with foliage, and the space round the arch panelled; the jambs ornamented with shafts, and the spandrels filled with shields and foliage.

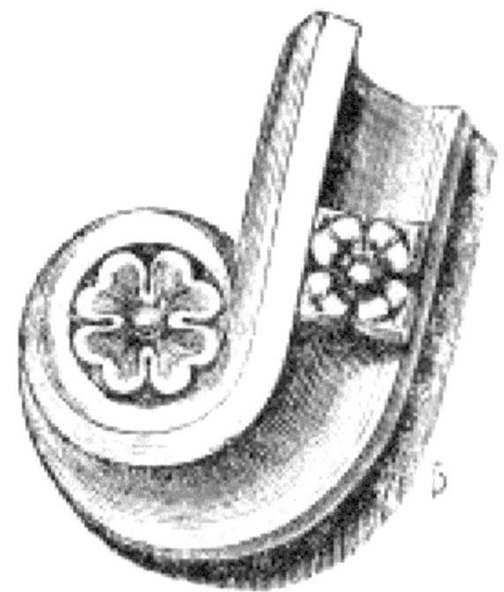

Dripstone termination, Rushden, Northants.

It has been mentioned that the old wooden door, with the original iron-work, frequently remains; a good instance of this occurs at Beckley Church, Oxon, which has the usual square-head and dripstone over it, with the dripstone terminations which are heads, probably, of the donors. This door is protected by a porch, and in the corner next the door is the niche for a stoup of holy-water, with which the people sprinkled themselves as they went into the church. This place for the stoup is frequently found just inside the door, instead of outside. The iron-work of this style is not so good as that of the Early English or Decorated, but still it is often very good, and is frequently preserved; it has the advantage of not requiring a porch to protect it, but was originally painted or gilt in some instances.

West Doorway, Fotheringhay, A.D. 1435.

The west doorway of the church of Fotheringhay is a very good example of this style, with the well-molded square head over it, the molded arch with shafts in the jambs and shields, and foliated circles in the spandrels.

THE TOWERS in this style are frequently extremely rich and elaborately ornamented, having four or five storeys of large windows with rich canopies, pinnacles, and tabernacles; double buttresses at the angles, and rich deep open parapets, with pinnacles and crocketed turrets at the corners, having small flying or hanging pinnacles attached. These very gorgeous towers are chiefly found in Somersetshire, as at Wrington, Taunton, Brislington, Dundry, &c. There are, however, few which, for beauty of proportion and chasteness of composition, can rival that of Magdalen College, Oxford. In that example the lower storeys are extremely plain, all the ornament being reserved for the belfry-windows, the parapet, and pinnacles; by this judicious arrangement the eye takes in the whole subject at once, thus giving to it a solemnity and a repose which are not attained by the more gorgeous specimens before referred to. This tower was originally intended to stand alone, as a campanile, or belfry-tower; the buildings which have been erected on two sides of it are of a subsequent period. At the time it was building, Wolsey, afterwards the celebrated Cardinal and Prime Minister of Henry VIII., was a Fellow of this College, and held the office of Bursar; *tradition* gives him the credit of the design, there is no better authority for this, but it is probably true he was a great builder.

Dundry, Bristol, c. A.D. 1520.   Magdalen College, Oxford, c. A.D. 1492.

The light and elegant style of vaulting known as fan-tracery[6], which is pecu-

[6] It should be noticed that fan-tracery vaulting is *peculiarly English*, the principle of it began with the earliest English Gothic style, as in the cloisters of Lincoln Cathedral, each stone of the vaulting being cut to fit its place. In France this is never done, each block of

liar to this style, with its delicate pendants and lace-like ornaments, harmonizes finely with the elaborate ornament of the tabernacle-work below.

THE PORCHES are in general very fine, and highly enriched with panel-work, buttresses, and pinnacles; open parapets, windows, and tabernacles with figures, flanking the window or the outer arch, and in the interior sometimes a richly-groined vault. Very fine examples of these porches are found in Norfolk, Somersetshire, Devonshire, and Dorsetshire.

There are frequently very good porches of this style of a more ordinary kind in the parish churches, with a stone vault, as at the west end of Woodstock, Oxon. This church had been partly rebuilt in the Georgian era, in the style of that period, on the side next the street; but at the back and at the end, where it is out of sight, the old work has been preserved in the complete restoration of this church in the time of Queen Victoria.

West Porch, Woodstock, Oxon, c. A.D. 1500.

In later examples we find ornament used to such an excess as completely to overpower the usual characteristic features of the building; no large space is left stone is oblong, as in those for the walls, and is only made to curve over in a vault by the mortar between the joints. This had the effect of making vaulting much cheaper to construct, and therefore much more abundant in France than in England, but it is always less scientific and often less beautiful; good French architects, with the late M. Viollet-le-Duc, much admired the English vaulting.

on which the eye can rest, but every portion is occupied with panelling or other ornament.

An example of this may be seen in the exterior of Henry the Seventh's Chapel, which has more the appearance of a piece of wood-carving than of a building of stone; but in the interior of the same building this very richness has a wonderfully fine effect.

THE MOLDINGS of this style differ much from the preceding ones. They are in general more shallow; that is, they have more breadth and less depth than the earlier ones. Those in most use are a wide and shallow molding, used in the jambs of windows and doorways, as in Haseley, No. 1; a shallow ogee; a round, or boutell; a fillet, a kind of hollow quarter-round, and a double ogee, as in Haseley, No. 2. The wide molding of cornices is sometimes filled up at intervals with large pateræ, which replace the four-leaved flower and the ball-flower of the Decorated style; or with heads, grotesque figures, or animals and foliage. These are frequently inferior both in conception and execution, to the earlier styles.

Tudor Flower, Henry the Seventh's Chapel.

There is an ornament which was introduced in this style, and which is very characteristic. This is called the "Tudor-flower," not because it was introduced in the time of the Tudors, but because it was so much used at that period. It generally consists of some modification of the fleur-de-lis, alternately with a small trefoil or ball, and is much used as a crest for screens, on fonts, niches, capitals, and in almost all places where such ornament can be used.

PERPENDICULAR MOLDINGS.

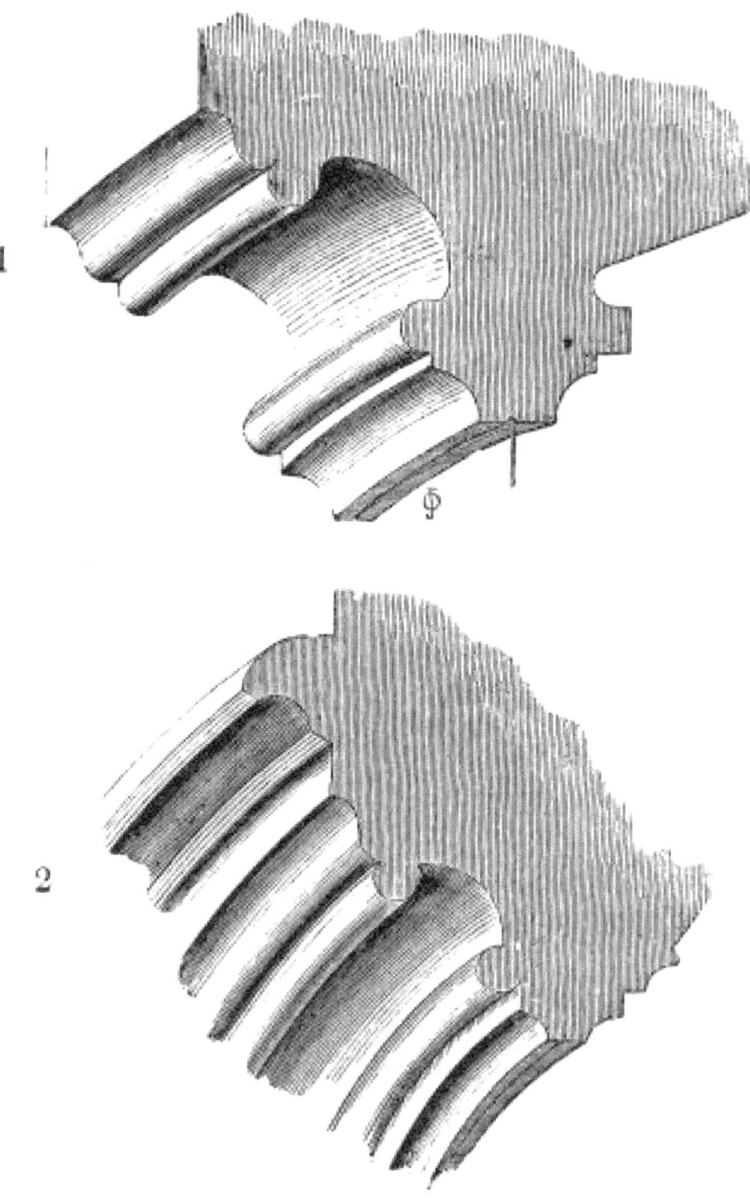

Haseley, Oxon, c. A.D. 1480.

The foliage of this style is frequently very beautifully executed, almost as faithful to nature as in the Decorated style, in which the fidelity to nature is one of the characteristic features. In Devonshire the foliage of the capitals is peculiar, often resembling a wreath of flowers twisted round the top of the pillar; and this may probably have been the idea of the sculptors, as the custom of decorating churches with flowers at certain seasons is a very ancient one; it is probable also that the sculpture was originally coloured after nature. There is comparatively a squareness about the Perpendicular foliage which takes from the freshness and beauty which distinguished that of the Decorated style. Indeed, the use of square and angular forms is one of the characteristics of the style; we have square panels, square foliage, square crockets and finials, square forms in the windows,—caused by the introduction of so many transoms,—and an approach to squareness in the depressed and low pitch of the roofs in late examples.

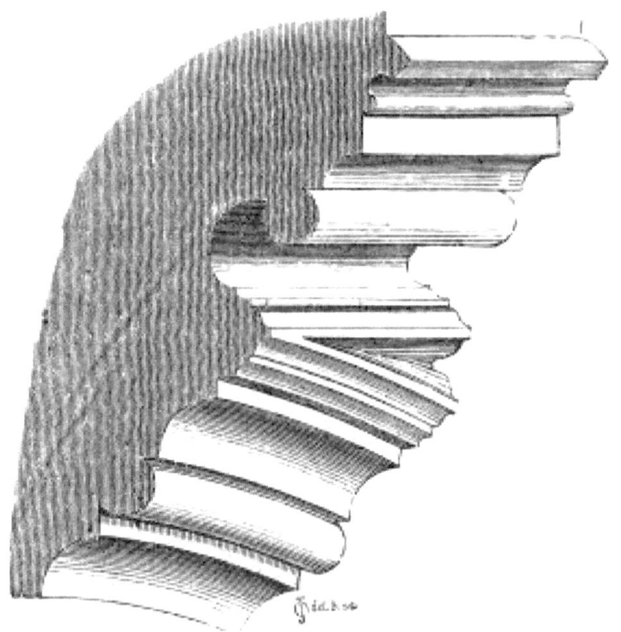

Doorway, Fotheringhay, Northants, A.D. 1435.

It is frequently said that it is not easy to distinguish the moldings of the Perpendicular style from those of the earlier styles, but this is in general because people do not pay attention to them. The moldings of Fotheringhay are particularly good, and they have a positive date, yet if these are compared with either of the earlier styles the difference is very evident. The hollows are more shallow, the projection not so bold, and these are the usual characteristics.

THE BUTTRESSES of this style do not differ materially from those of the Decorated, but the triangular heads to the different stages are less frequently used; the set-offs are more frequently plain slopes only. The projection of buttresses of this style is usually greater than in any of the previous styles, especially in those that have to support towers, when there are commonly three stages, sometimes more, and they are often placed diagonally at the corners, or there are two, one on either side of the corner. Sometimes a buttress of this style is very thin, and has two diagonal faces; there is frequently a niche on the face of the buttress, either for an image, which seldom remains, or for a shield of arms only, and this more often remains. Sometimes there is a half-arch through the lower part of the buttress, as at Gloucester, and this is quite distinct from the flying buttress, the object of which usually is to support the wall of the clere-storey, by carrying the pressure across the roof of the aisle on to the outer wall, and on these pinnacles are placed over each buttress, the direct outward weight of the pinnacle serving to counteract the side pressure, as at Fotheringhay.

Flying Buttresses, Fotheringhay, Northants, A.D. 1435.

In this excellent example it will at once be seen that the upper end of each of the arch-buttresses must catch the lower end of the timbers of the roof, and so conveys the pressure to the outer wall, where again the weight of the vertical pinnacle helps to counteract the side pressure of the arch-buttress. There is also a massive part of the buttress against the lower wall.

Empty niches for images are very abundant in this style, but it is rare to find the figure left in the niches that were made for it; they do occur occasionally, and are sometimes almost as good as those of the preceding style. There is a very good one in the tower of S. Mary Magdalen Church, Oxford, which is believed to have been brought from the ruins of Osney Abbey, as that tower is of the time of Henry VIII.

S. Mary Magdalen, Oxford, c. A.D. 1500.

The figure of the patron saint over the outer door of the porch of a parish church has frequently been preserved; occasionally the figures in the niches of a churchyard cross still remain.

Corbel, Rushden, c. A.D. 1500.

The frequent use of figures, simply as corbels between the windows of the clere-storey to carry the roof, is a good characteristic of the late Perpendicular style; they are generally of the time of Henry the Seventh or Eighth, as at Rushden, Northants. The figure used is generally that of an angel, and each angel is some-times represented as carrying a different musical instrument, so as to make up a heavenly choir. In this instance the instrument carried is one sometimes called a mouth-organ, or shepherd's pipes.

The splendid Open Timber Roofs, as at St. Stephen's Church, Norwich, which are the glory of the eastern counties, belong almost entirely to this style; the screens and lofts across the chancel-arch, and often across the aisles also, and the richly carved bench-ends for which the West of England is so justly celebrated, also belong to it; in fact, nearly the whole of the medieval woodwork which we have remaining is of this style, and this material appears to be peculiarly adapted for it. It may reasonably be doubted whether the modern attempts to revive the woodwork of the Norman and Early English styles are not altogether a mistake. Nothing can well exceed the richness and beauty of the Perpendicular woodwork, and it is easy to imagine that a church of the twelfth or thirteenth century has been newly furnished in the fifteenth or sixteenth. We have, however, some very beautiful examples of Decorated woodwork in screens, and stalls with their canopies, as at Winchester; there are also a few wooden tombs of that period.

In Norfolk there are several fine examples remaining of galleries and screens, commonly called roodlofts, being used at the west end of the church also, under the tower, and across the tower-arch; and this in churches where the roodloft, properly so called, still remains across the chancel-arch, so that there is a quasi-roodloft at each end of the nave.

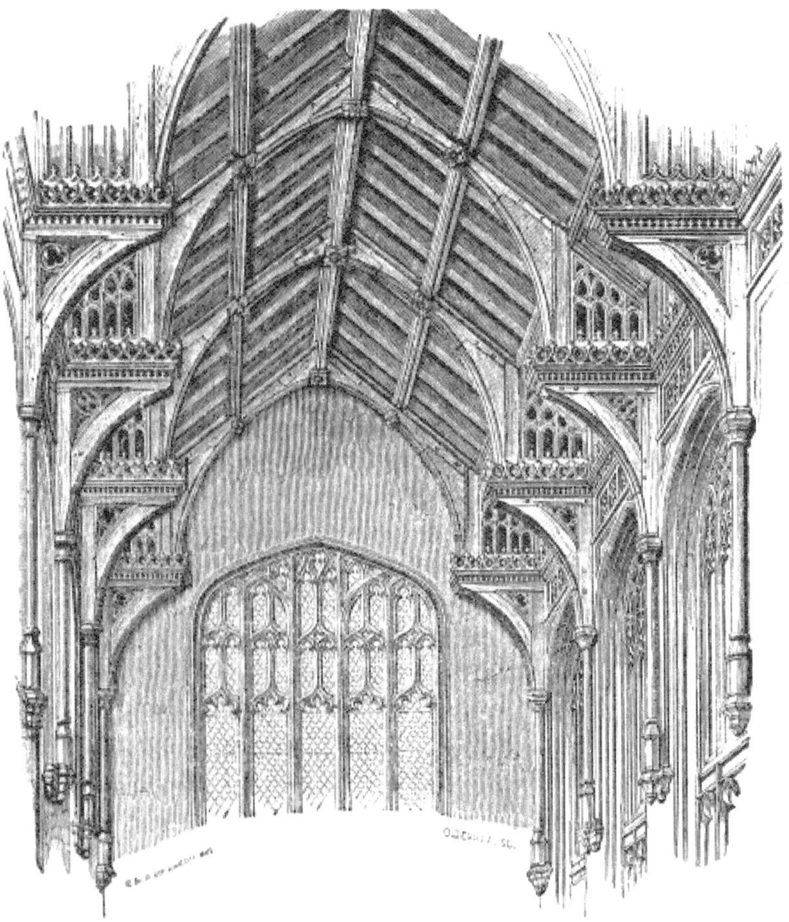

St. Stephen's Church, Norwich, c. A.D. 1500.

There is no doubt that this custom prevailed in many other counties also, but the western loft has generally been destroyed in consequence of the barbarous custom of blocking up the tower-arch, which is often the finest feature in the church. The roodloft-galleries seem to have been used for choristers to stand upon; the lessons were also read from them. They are sometimes very large, extending over the eastern bay of the nave and occasionally over the western bay of the chancel also, as may be seen by the remains of the staircases for them.

The Redcliffe Church, Bristol, the west front and south porch of Gloucester Cathedral, and part of the choir of St. Alban's Abbey Church, with the tomb of Abbot Wheathampstead, are also of this period, and good specimens of the style. Within the next twenty years we have a crowd of examples, which it is not necessary to enumerate.

But a few more specimens of the later period of this style can hardly be passed over, such as St. George's Chapel, Windsor, King's College Chapel, Cambridge, and Henry the Seventh's Chapel, Westminster; and of the very latest before the change of style, Bath Abbey Church, the Savoy Chapel, in the Strand, London, with its very beautiful panelled ceiling, and Whiston Church, Northants.

GOTHIC ARCHITECTURE is usually considered to have come to an end in England in the time of Henry VIII. This is only *partially true*, it lingered on in many districts for another century; this was especially the case in Oxford, and I have much pleasure in republishing an excellent memoir on this subject by the late Mr. Orlando Jewitt, read at the meeting of the Royal Archæological Institute at Oxford, in 1850. It has never been much circulated, and has been quite forgotten, but the facts speak for themselves, and are clearly stated by Mr. Jewitt, and proved by his admirable woodcuts of these buildings. He was a thorough artist, and an enthusiastic lover of the subject of Gothic Architecture. His woodcuts differ from any others in this respect, they are not made from drawings, but are drawn on the wood by himself from the objects, and then handed to his brother, Henry Jewitt, to be engraved; the latter long had the reputation of "being able to cut the finest line of any one in the trade," and in wood-engraving, where the lines have to be left standing to be printed, and the other parts to become white surface, cut away, the finest lines necessarily produce the finest woodcuts.

Some people talk of the Elizabethan and Jacobean style, but this is really no style at all, any more than what is foolishly called "the Queen Anne style." All of these are jumbles of various styles, they are neither Gothic, nor Grecian, nor Roman, nor Italian, but can only be called with truth a *mongrel* mixture of styles, to which various names are given for convenience. The idea that they are *cheaper* on this account is entirely a delusion; the same amount of space to be covered, and the same extent of walls and of ornament, will cost the same whatever *the style* may be; that is a matter of taste only, about which it is needless to dispute; if any people are so blind as to prefer this mongrel work to a genuine style there is no help for it, they must expose themselves to the ridicule of the next generation.

The Gothic Architecture of Oxford, even as late as the seventeenth century, was not in this mongrel style, it was as good as the generality of modern Gothic of the Victorian school. The fan-tracery vault over the staircase of the hall of Christ Church, for instance, carried on a central pillar, as in a mediæval chapter-house, is thoroughly good Gothic, although the only record that we have of it is that it was built by "one Smith, an artificer from London," in the time of Charles the Second. In the county of Somerset also there are some excellent examples of very late Gothic, and in some other districts; the English people were not willing to give up their preference for this their own national style to any other.

ON THE LATE, OR DEBASED, GOTHIC BUILDINGS OF OXFORD. FROM THE REIGN OF ELIZABETH TO THE END OF THE SEVENTEENTH CENTURY.

GOTHIC ARCHITECTURE seems to have attained its ultimate perfection in the fourteenth century, at which period everything belonging to it was conceived and executed in a free and bold spirit, all the forms were graceful and natural, and all the details of foliage and other sculptures were copied from living types, with a skill and truth of drawing which has never been surpassed. Conventional forms were in a great measure abandoned, and it seems to have been rightly and truly considered that the fittest monuments for the House of God were faithful copies of His works; and so long as this principle continued to be acted on, so long did Gothic Architecture remain pure. But in the succeeding century, under the later Henries and Edwards, a gradual decline took place: everything was molded to suit a preconceived idea, the foliage lost its freshness, and was molded into something of a rectangular form; the arches were depressed, the windows lowered, the flowing curves of the tracery converted into straight lines, panelling profusely used, and the square form everywhere introduced; until at length the prevalence of the horizontal line led easily and naturally to the *renaissance* of the classic styles, though in an impure and much degraded form. The mixture of the two styles first appears in the time of Henry VII.,—a period in which (though remarkable for the beauty and delicacy of its details) the grand conceptions of form and proportion of the previous century seem to have been lost. Heaviness or clumsiness of form, combined with exquisite beauty of detail, are the characteristics of this era.

In the time of Henry VIII. the details became debased, and there was a great mixture of Italian work, but still the Gothic ideas predominated, and there are some good examples of this date remaining, of which the Hall of Christ Church may be adduced as a proof.

In the reign of Elizabeth the mixture of the two styles was more complete; and though the details were frequently incongruous, there resulted from the union a style which, when applied to domestic buildings, was highly picturesque, and occasionally produced great richness of effect[7].

---

[7] A curious example of Elizabethan work occurs at Sunningwell Church, within a few miles of Oxford, where there is a singular polygonal porch at the west end, being a mixture of Ionic columns and Gothic windows. There is also some good woodwork of the same period. The church was chiefly rebuilt by Bishop Jewel.

In the succeeding period the decline still continued; feature after feature was lost, until at length all was swallowed up by its rival. That feature, however, which was always the most important and most characteristic of Gothic architecture, and on which at all periods the distinctions of the styles chiefly depended, namely, the window, was the last to depart; for when every other trace of the style was lost, we find the windows still retaining either their Gothic form or their Gothic tracery, and thus evincing the lingering love which was still felt for the ancient forms.

During all this period of decline, however, frequent attempts were made to stay its progress, and in no place more successfully than in Oxford, as the number of buildings of this period will testify. To point out the peculiarities, and to give the most remarkable points of the history of these buildings, will be the subject of the present paper, the historical facts of which are taken chiefly from Dr. Ingram's "Memorials of Oxford," and from Anthony à Wood.

The first building of this period which claims attention is the Bodleian Library, and in order to understand the history of this, it will be necessary to go a little farther back. It seems that various donations of books had been made by different individuals in the thirteenth and fourteenth centuries, but that no proper depository had been provided for them, and that they remained either locked up in chests or chained to desks in the old Congregation-house, and in the various chapels of St. Mary's Church, until a room or "solar" having been built for them by Bishop Cobham in 1320, over the old Congregation-house[8], they were, after various disputes, removed there in 1409. It seems, too, that the University had at this time fallen into great irregularity, and suffered great inconvenience from the want of public authorised schools; the various professors using for that purpose apartments in private houses in various parts of the city.

This led to the erection of a building for that purpose in 1439; and about the same time the University resolved to erect a separate School for Divinity on a large scale, in a central situation near the other schools. Liberal contributions having been made by various persons, and especially by Humphrey, Duke of Gloucester, son of Henry IV., they were enabled, about the year 1480, not only to complete the Divinity School as it now stands, but to build the room over it for a library; and from the circumstance of the Duke being the principal donor, both in his lifetime and at his death, and of his bequeathing a number of valuable manuscripts, he is styled the founder, and the Library was called by his name. Into this Library the books from St. Mary's were removed[9].

---

[8] By a curious coincidence, the old Congregation-house, on the north side of the chancel of St. Mary's Church, has been converted into the "Chapel for the Unattached Students."

[9] The workmen employed were the same as were employed at Eton and Windsor, under the direction of William of Waynfleet, and were called away from Oxford under a royal mandate, but were restored again in consequence of a petition from the University.

GOTHIC BUILDINGS OF OXFORD.

East Window, Bodleian Library, A.D. 1610, inserted in the older panelling.

The Divinity School yet remains in much the same state as when built, except that a doorway was made by Sir Christopher Wren, under one of the windows on the north side for the convenience of processions to the Theatre, and that at the east end the doorway has been altered externally. On examination, it will be found that the outer moldings have been cut down even with the wall; and from the marks on the wall, it seems probable that there was a groined porch projecting in this direction, and that this was removed to make way for the covered walk, or Proscholium, when the Bodleian Library was built.

Imposts, Proscholium of the Divinity School.

After the Reformation, the schools appear for some years to have been almost deserted and in ruins, until, in the reign of Elizabeth, in the year 1597, Sir Thomas Bodley, a gentleman of a Devonshire family, who had been educated in the University, (and who had afterwards travelled through most parts of Europe, and been employed by Queen Elizabeth in many important matters,) resolved, as he tells us himself, to "set up his staff at the Library-door at Oxford," and restore the place to the use of students. He commenced the same year the restoration of Duke Humphrey's Library, which he repaired and refitted, and to which he added a new roof; and afterwards, in 1610, commenced building the Library which now bears his name, but which he did not live to see finished[10]. This new building he

---

[10] The architect employed was Thomas Holt of York, who was likewise employed

placed at the east end of, and transversely to, the Divinity School, the north-east and south-east buttresses being built into the new wall, and leaving in front of the east door the Proscholium or covered walk already mentioned, popularly known as the "Pig-market." Of this Wood says, "In which Ambulachrum do stand such that are candidates for, or sue after, their graces to the Regents sitting in the Congregation House adjoining." The reason of this being, that any requisite questions might be put to them previous to granting the degrees,—a practice which was discontinued when the system of public examinations was introduced[11].

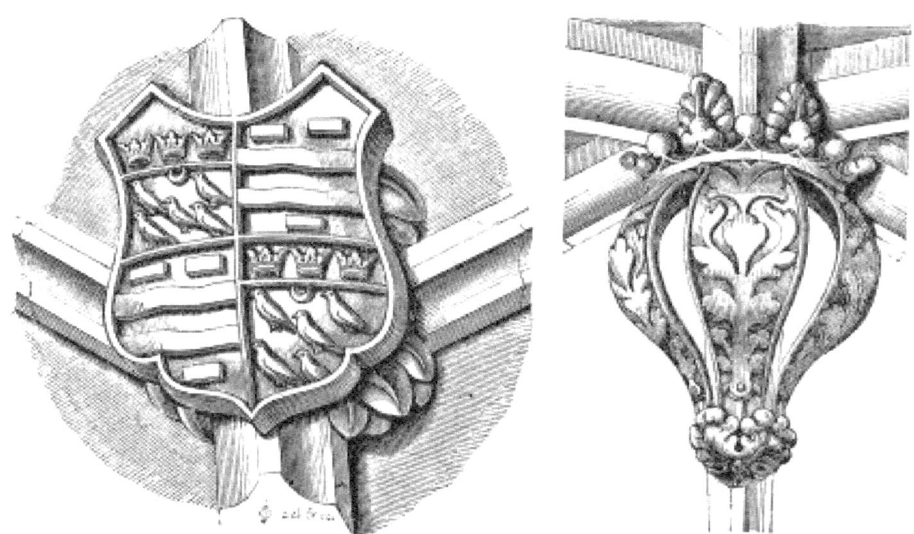

Bosses, Proscholium of the Divinity School.

It was necessary, therefore, in making the new building, to retain this space, and the present groined room was formed accordingly. It is lighted by a window at each end, one of which is not, nor has ever been intended to be, glazed. It has a vaulted ceiling, with bosses at the intersections, the alternate ones being shields, with the arms of the founder[12]. Some of the bosses are of good design and execution, but others are of late character. The general effect is good, but the details,

over several of the other buildings in Oxford at the same period. He died in 1624, and was buried in Holywell Churchyard. The builders were first, J. Acroid, who died in 1613; and afterwards J. Bentley, who built likewise the new buildings of Merton, and M. Bentley, who died in 1618.

[11] From this arose the popular, but erroneous belief that the candidates were compelled to walk an hour in the Pig-market, in order to allow the tradesmen to whom they were indebted to recognise them, and obtain payment of their debts, it being a rule that no candidate against whom an action for debt is pending in the University court, can receive a degree. But though the belief was not correct, it was until a comparatively recent period the custom for tradesmen to attend at those times for the purpose mentioned.

[12] Quarterly, 1 and 4, Argent five martlets saltier-wise sable; on a chief azure, three ducal coronets, Or; a crescent for difference.—*Bodley*. 2 and 3, Argent, two bars wavy, between three billets sable.—*Hore*.

particularly the moldings, are of very debased character.

The buttresses of the Divinity School are panelled the greater part of their height, and one of these, as has been mentioned before, is built in, and forms part of Bodley's new wall, so that the panelling is visible on both sides; but on the east end it is carried forward on the face of the wall, as far as the point from which the porch seems to have projected; and it is tolerably evident, from the remains of the shafts which have been cut away, and from other marks on the wall, that this porch must have been groined. It seems to have been the wish of Bodley to have his new building to agree in character with the old, and he therefore had the whole of his building panelled in the same manner as the Divinity School. This forms the west side of the Schools' Quadrangle[13], and is different in character from the rest of the buildings. The width of the quadrangle of the schools is greater than the length of the front of the Bodleian, and therefore a few feet had to be added at each end of Bodley's work. This may be seen inside these staircases, particularly between the entrances to the Bodleian and the Picture Gallery, where the old work is panelled, and has a corbel-table the same as the rest of the front, but the new work is plain. The upper storey of this building joins Duke Humphrey's Library, and is lighted by a large window at each end, and another opposite the old library. This window is a curious combination of mullions, transoms, and tracery of different forms. The rest of the windows are small.

---

[13] The two staircases were added afterwards, but were panelled to match the rest of the work. On the north end this panelling seems to have been subsequently cut away, so that nothing but the small arches remain attached to the under side of the strings. In Williams's *Oxonia Depicta* it is shewn completely panelled.

Staircase and Doorways of the Bodleian Library and Picture Gallery.

Shewing the junction of Bodley's work with the older panelling.

Sir Thomas Bodley, shortly before his death, had conceived and matured the plan of a new building for the Public Schools of the University, and everything was settled for carrying the plan into execution; but he did not live to see it commenced. He died at his house in London in 1613, his body was brought to Oxford, and buried in Merton College Chapel on the 29th of March in that year; and the day after the funeral the first stone of the new Schools was laid, the building of which occupied the next six years.

GOTHIC BUILDINGS OF OXFORD.

Groining, Gateway of the Schools, A.D. 1610.

This building, which, with the Bodleian Library for its west side, forms a complete quadrangle, is plain, poor, and heavy in its general appearance, and little skill has been displayed in giving either variety of outline or of light and shade. This plainness is still further increased by the removal of the transoms with which the windows were originally furnished, and which are still retained in those in the tower. The Gateway-tower on the east side, which afforded an opportunity for this, is not distinguished by any projection from the flat wall, but merely rises above the parapet on the same plane. The oriel, too, over the doorway, which might have given effect, is tame and poor. The whole mass is square, without buttresses or any other projection to relieve it. In the inner front of the Tower, however, more pains have been taken; the five storeys into which it is divided are each ornamented with columns of one of the five classic orders, the plinths, friezes, and the shafts, for a third of their length, being covered with the peculiar Arabesque of the period, intermixed with the national emblems, &c. In the fourth storey is a figure of James

I., and the whole is surmounted with a parapet of open scroll-work enclosing the royal arms. These figures were originally gilt. Taken altogether, this composition is a favourable specimen of the style of that time, though it does not harmonise with the Gothic turret and pinnacle which rise above it. The archway is groined, and is a curious example, the bosses being all more or less of Elizabethan design.

Central Boss, Gateway of the Schools.

The wooden door is panelled, the panels being filled with the arms of the various colleges as late as Wadham, that being then newly-erected.

Anthony à Wood's description of this gateway is so good in its way, and harmonises so completely with his subject, that it is here given complete: —

"But between the geometry and metaphysic, and astronomy and logic schools, is the chief entrance from Cat Street into this new fabric; having over it an eminent and stately tower, wherein are contained, beside the vault or entrance, four rooms; the first is the mathematical library for the use of the Savilian professors; the second is part of the gallery; the third, the muniments and registers of the University; and the fourth, which is the uppermost, doth serve for astronomy uses. On the outside of the said tower, next to the area, or quadrangle, is beheld the rise of five stories of pillars (equal to every storey of the tower), viz., of Thuscan, Doric, Ionic, Corinthian, and Composite work. Between the upper storey of pillars saving one is the effigies of King James I. cut very curiously in stone, sitting on a throne, and giving with his right hand a book to the picture or emblem of Fame, with this inscription on the cover:

"HÆC HABEO QUÆ SCRIPSI.

"With his left hand he reacheth out another book to our mother, the University of Oxford, represented in effigie, kneeling to the King, with this inscription on the cover also:

"HÆC HABEO QUÆ DEDI.

"On the verge of the canopy over the throne, and the King's head, which is also most admirably cut in stone, is his motto:

"BEATI PACIFICI.

"Over that also are emblems of Justice, Peace and Plenty, and underneath all, this inscription in golden letters:

"REGNANTE D. JACOBO REGUM DOCTISSIMO
MUNIFICENTISSIMO, OPTIMO, HÆ MUSIS
EXTRUCTÆ MOLES, CONGESTA BIBLIOTHECA,
ET QUÆCUNQUE ADHUC DEERANT AD SPLENDOREM
ACADEMIÆ FELICITER TENTATA,
COEPTA ABSOLUTA. SOLI DEO GLORIA.

"All which Pictures and Emblems were at first with great cost and splendour double gilt; but when K. James came from Woodstock to see this quadrangular pile, commanded them (being so glorious and splendid that none, especially when the sun shines, could behold them) to be whited over, and adorned with ordinary colours, which hath since so continued." — Vol. iii. p. 793.

An addition was made at the west end of the Divinity School, 1634 to 1640, the lower part of which is the Convocation House, and the upper part an addition to the library for containing the books of the learned Selden, and is called by his name.

The next building in order of time is Wadham College, which was commenced in 1610, and finished in 1613, the year in which the Schools were commenced. It was founded by Sir Nicholas and Dame Dorothy Wadham, (whose effigies appear over the doorway of the hall,) but was not begun until after the death of Sir Nicholas in 1609. The building was commenced in 1610, and the whole of the quadrangle, the hall and chapel, were completed in 1613.

The general character of the buildings of the quadrangle is the same as that of the Schools, having a tower-gateway, and oriel-window in the same situation; but the hall and ante-chapel are of somewhat different character, having debased tracery in the windows formed of scroll-work, and of which the large window of the hall is a very curious example. But the most singular part is the chapel, which is totally different in style from the rest of the buildings; the windows have good Perpendicular tracery and moldings, though of rather late character, and there is little to distinguish it from a pure Perpendicular building, except the upper moldings of the buttresses, In the east window, however, there is a singularity in the subordination of the tracery, which would not have occurred in the best period of Perpendicular. The two mullions of the centre light are carried through the head and on each side in the sub-arches. The other two mullions are not carried through, but another rises from the second and fourth lights, cutting through the sub-arches; and by this means the primary tracery, not being equally distributed over the space, produces an awkward effect, though the window has evidently, but not skilfully, been copied from those of New College. The side-windows are of three lights with transoms, and are good in all their details; and there are in the interior two lofty arches, which divide the ante-chapel from the transept, and which are of the same character, and are also an imitation of those in New College. The rest of the ante-chapel corresponds with the hall, so that it produces one uniform front towards the quadrangle. The character of this part is totally different to that of the chapel; and the contrast of the two (shewn in the woodcut on p. 239), is very striking. The tracery of the one is good Perpendicular, but that of the other is of a kind unknown to Gothic. It is composed of scroll-work in elliptic forms, and with a kind of flat bosses at the intersections. The moldings, too, are totally different, one not differing much from the usual section of a Perpendicular window, and the other non-descript, as will be seen from the sections.

GOTHIC BUILDINGS OF OXFORD.

Arches of the Ante-chapel, Wadham College, A.D. 1610-13.

Sections of Windows of the Chapel and Ante-Chapel, Wadham College, A.D. 1610-13.

GOTHIC BUILDINGS OF OXFORD.

Windows of the Chapel and Ante-chapel, Wadham College, A.D. 1610-13.

These striking differences have naturally induced a belief that the chapel was either a prior erection, or that the old materials of the Augustine convent, on the site of which the college was built, had been used up again; but by the investigations of the Rev. J. Griffith, whose valuable paper on the subject gives the accounts referred to, it is clearly shewn that the building of the two parts was carried on simultaneously. The foundress seems to have had a proper idea that a building used for Divine service should have a different character from those which were intended for domestic uses, and therefore, as the regular masons at that period could not have been much used to church-work, and as it is shewn by the accounts[14] that the masons employed were brought to Oxford from a distance, it seems probable that she brought, from her own county of Somerset, workmen who had been used to this kind of work. The churches of Somersetshire are mostly of rich and late Perpendicular character, and it is probable that the style might continue later there than in other places. It would, therefore, be a curious subject to inquire if any churches were built so late as that on which these masons might have been employed. The Hall of Wadham has an open timber roof, which is curious, as shewing how, while the Gothic form was retained, the details were altered to suit the taste of the times. The large window is a remarkable example of Jacobean tracery.

---

[14] In these accounts, (for an opportunity of examining which I am indebted to the Rev. J. Griffith, Sub-Warden [now, in 1881, the Warden]), the masons who worked the stone for building are called *Free* masons, or *Freestone Masons* (which is probably the true meaning of the term), while the rest are merely called "labourers." The cost of each window, with the name of the workman, is put down separately, the price of a chapel window being 6*l.*, while those of the hall were 3*l.* 18*s.* each. It is curious, too, to find that the three statues over the entrance to the hall and chapel were cut by one of the free masons (William Blackshaw) employed on the other parts of the building. For each statue he was paid the sum of 3*l.*

The following prices and terms also appear, and are curious and interesting, [but great allowance must be made for the change in the value of money; it is probable that each shilling of the time of James I. was equivalent to at least ten shillings in the time of Queen Victoria]: —

Lodgement, 4d. per foot.

Window table, 4d. per foot.

Grass table, 4d. per foot.

Window lights, 3s. 4d. each.

Pillar stone, at 16d. per foot.

Cornish, 2d. per foot.

Gorgel table

Gargill

Gurgul

Gurgoll

—at 4d. per foot.

Tun stone, or tun stuff

Tounel stones, or tunnel stones

—stones for chimney shafts, &c.

The entrance under the principal gateway is groined, with fan-vaulting, having in the centre the arms of the founder and foundress impaled.

The buildings of this period in Oxford are very numerous; indeed there are few colleges which have not some additions of this time; but it will not be necessary to do much more than enumerate the most favourable examples, with their dates.

The inner quadrangle of Merton College is stated to have been built by J. Bentley, one of the builders of the Schools, and the gateway into the gardens is an evident imitation of that of the Schools. It has four of the orders, and the spaces between are filled with Gothic panelling, but the effect is poor and flat. The external front of this part, which faces Merton, is, however, a very good composition, and embowered as it is with trees, has quite the character of one of the fine old mansions of the Elizabethan or Jacobean period.

The Hall of Trinity College, built in 1618 to 1620, has good Perpendicular windows.

Jesus College Chapel, built in 1621, and the east window of the chapel, which was added in 1636, are much better than might have been expected at the period, but there is no subordination of tracery, which all springs from the same fillet.

East Window, Jesus College, A.D. 1636.

The Chapel of Exeter College, built in 1624 [since rebuilt], was a better specimen than the last. The tracery of the windows seems to have been copied from New College, and the subordination is preserved. The door, however, is completely of Jacobean character.

The second quadrangle of St. John's, which was built by Archbishop Laud between 1631 and 1636, is remarkable, and different from anything else in Oxford. It is by Inigo Jones, and the effect of the garden front is highly picturesque, and the combination of the Gothic forms with Elizabethan details skilfully managed. This mixture of styles, though it will not bear examination in detail, produces in the mass an effect highly pleasing; and harmonising so well as it does with the foliage by which it is surrounded, it seems well suited for the purpose for which it is here employed. The quadrangle is on two sides supported on Doric columns and arches, the spandrels of which are filled with heads, and with emblems of the sciences and of the moral virtues.

The Hall and Chapel of St. Mary Hall were built between the years 1632 and

1644. The arrangement is curious and unusual, the hall occupying the lower storey, and the chapel the upper. The windows of the hall are square-headed, but those of the chapel on the north and south sides are round-headed, with intersecting tracery. The filling-up of the heads of the lights is singular. The tracery, which assumes something of a Flamboyant form, springs from the chamfer in the manner of a cusp, and its fillets do not touch in the middle. The east window is pointed, and of five lights, with a mixture of intersecting and Perpendicular tracery, the whole exhibiting a good example of that commingling of preceding styles which is so frequently found in late Gothic structures.

Entrance to the Chapel, Exeter College, A.D. 1624 [in A.D. 1861]

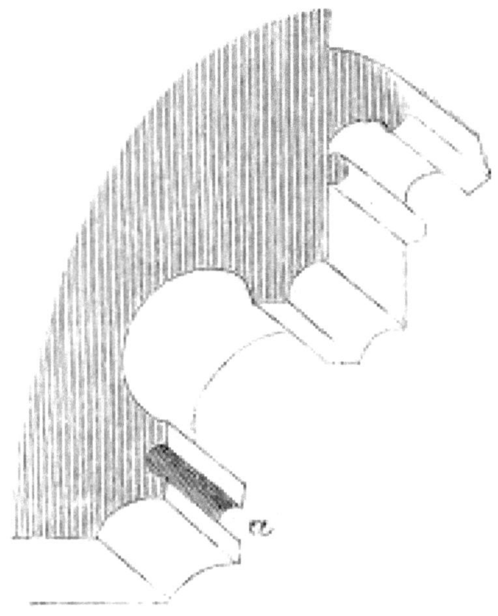

Section of Window, Lincoln College Chapel, A.D. 1631.

a. Grooved Fillet.

The Chapel of Lincoln College was built in 1631, and is one of the best examples of the period; the subordination of the tracery is preserved, and the moldings are good, except one peculiarity, which seems to belong to this period, as it is found likewise at Oriel and other places. This is,—the fillet is left broad, and is grooved down the centre with a rather deep channel. This has the effect of dividing the fillet into two lines, and produces a clumsy appearance.

Oriel College was built about 1620, but the Hall and Chapel were begun in 1637, and finished in 1642. The character of the building is poor and clumsy. The tracery is of very late character, and it has the grooved fillet above mentioned. The entrance to the chapel is under a bay-window, which has an open parapet of scroll-work.

East Window, St. Mary Hall, A.D. 1644.

In this instance the form of the arch of the window, the character of the moldings, and the arrangement of the tracery, are better than was usual at that late period.

The windows of the Hall and Chapel of University College, which were built about 1640, are much like those of Oriel. The east window of the chapel is particularly bad. Both colleges are built with fractable gablets.

In the Chapel of Brasenose College, which was built between 1656 and 1666, all traces of Gothic, except the windows and roof, seem to have vanished. The exterior is Corinthian, with pointed windows inserted between the pilasters. The tracery is of rather early form, and the whole is a very incongruous mixture. In the east and west windows even the tracery is altered, and the oval form introduced, so that this may be taken as one of the last and most curious examples of the decline of Gothic before its extinction. The roof of the chapel, which is a kind of hammer-beam with fan-vaulting above, was brought from the chapel of St. Mary's College, which formerly stood in the Corn Market, and which was founded by Henry VI. in 1435. This kind of vaulting seems to have retained its hold longer than any other feature of the Gothic styles, unless it be the windows. It is extensively used in Oxford under gateways and other small spaces, as at Wadham, University, St. John's, &c., but the finest specimen of it is the beautiful staircase to the Hall of Christ Church; and it is remarkable to find that it was erected so late as 1640; but it is stated by Peshall to have been built by Dean Fell, "by the help of — — Smith, an artificer of London." Who Smith of London may have been, or whether he executed any other works beside this, does not seem to have been ascertained; but certainly this work alone, executed at a time when Gothic Architecture everywhere else was sunk in utter debasement, ought to rescue his name from oblivion. Its chief fault is a want of boldness in the ribs, but this flatness was a fault of the time, which he did not overcome.

Side Window, St. Mary Hall, A.D. 1640.

In this example the debased character usual at that period comes out more distinctly than in the previous example, the arch of the window has entirely lost any point, and the tracery is very confused and irregular.

It has been generally considered that the whole of the work outside of the Hall was of this date, but it will be evident on examination that the two open doorways opposite the Hall-door, as well as the arches and doorways under the landing, are of Wolsey's time; all the details and the boldness of the work shew them to belong to his building. The parts, therefore, which Smith executed were the central pillar, and the vaulting which it supports, the steps, and parapets. This part, it seems, was left unfinished by Wolsey. The steps were not completed, and it was not roofed. It is, therefore, possible, as this design harmonises so well with the rest of the building, that the original drawings might have been preserved, and the present staircase built from them; but whoever was the designer, it stands as one of the most beautiful things in Oxford, and one which no visitor should omit seeing.

The buildings hitherto described or mentioned are all in Oxford, but there is another in its immediate neighbourhood which is worth notice; this is Water Eaton, a house which appears to have been built in the beginning of James I.'s reign, and to have been the residence of Lord Lovelace. It is now a farm-house, but remains in a perfect and almost unaltered state. The house has transomed windows and a projecting porch, ornamented with pillars and pilasters. It has a large court-yard, with a detached building for offices on each side of the gateway in front. On the north side of the court-yard is the chapel, having a yard on the south side. It is this building which is remarkable, as it remains almost in the same state as when built, the screen, pulpit, and open seats being the same as when first put in, and the building, though late, has scarcely any mixture of the later style.

The plan consists of a nave and chancel, divided by a chancel-arch and screen, and having diagonal buttresses at all the angles. There are no windows on the north side, but on the south the nave has two, and the chancel one; and there are an east and west window, and a door on the south side. The doorway is pointed under a square label. The arches of the windows are much depressed, but slightly pointed; the lights are foliated and carried up to the head without tracery. The east window has five lights, and the others three lights each. The moldings are of late character, but not debased; the bell-cot and cross are modern.

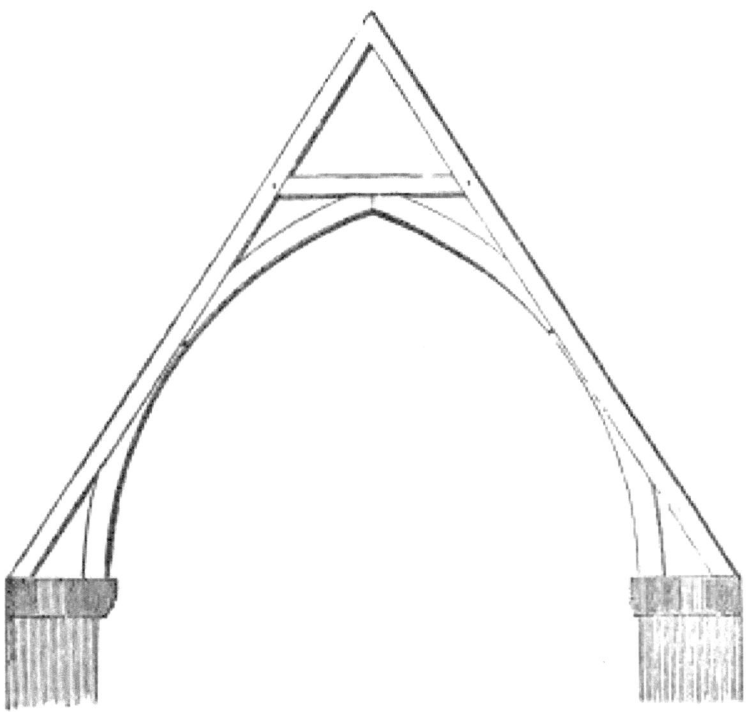

Roof of Chapel, Water Eaton, Oxon.

The construction of this roof is very good, and quite of the genuine mediæval or Gothic character, better than many roofs of the Victorian era.

The interior is very plain; the chancel-arch is semicircular, without moldings, but has a screen closed with doors; this is in the taste of the times, and is formed of semicircular arches, supported by small pillars, the whole carved with Elizabethan ornaments. The pulpit is a good specimen of this same style. The standards of the open seats are, as is usual at this period, rude, clumsy, and massive, the poppies being in imitation of the more ancient fleur-de-lis. The roof is a copy of an early form, and consists of principals, collar and curved braces, very plain and simple, but producing a good effect.

This building is interesting from shewing that here, as at Wadham College before mentioned, though the house was built in the revived manner, it was still thought necessary to keep the chapel in the old style, that being considered even then as exclusively ecclesiastical.

In the foregoing remarks, though very imperfectly executed, it has been intended to shew by the buildings of Oxford, not only the gradual decline of Gothic Architecture, but also the attempts, more or less successful, which were made from time to time to stay its progress. It was, however, for a time doomed to perish, and no efforts could save it. In the buildings of the period following that which has here been spoken of, it is either wholly laid aside, or the only remains of it are to be found in the accidental insertion, as it were, of a traceried window or a pointed door, as if to shew that some faint recollections of the once-honoured forms still lingered in the minds of the architects, and caused them involuntarily to record their respect for it.

It would be an interesting investigation to trace the gradual awakening of the style from the deep slumber into which it had fallen, and to trace its gradual unfolding, step by step, until we have at length a more glorious *rénaissance* of the Gothic styles than we ever had of the Classic; and in this history no mean place would be assigned to the Architectural Society of Oxford.

O. Jewitt.

The following list will form an useful appendix to the foregoing: —

Late Gothic Buildings in Oxford, from the Reign of Elizabeth to the End of the Seventeenth Century.

Eliz.	1571.	The old buildings of Jesus College commenced.
	1596.	Library, St. John's College, built.
	1597.	Sir Thomas Bodley commenced the repairs of Duke Humphrey's Library, and added the new roof.
	1600.	Front of St. Alban Hall built.
	1602.	Nov. 8. Duke Humphrey's Library publicly re-opened after the repairs.
Jas. I.	1610.	July 16. First stone of the Bodleian Library and Proscholium laid.
	1610.	Great or main quadrangle of Merton built.
	1610.	July 31. First stone of Wadham College laid.
	1612.	West side of the lesser quadrangle of Lincoln College built.
	1613.	March 30. First stone of the Schools laid.
	1613.	April 20. Wadham College opened.
	1617.	Hall of Jesus College built.
	1620.	Hall of Trinity College finished.
	1621.	May 28. Chapel of Jesus College consecrated.
	1624.	Chapel of Exeter College built.

Cｈ. I. 1626. Library of Jesus College built.

1628. Front of the house in St. Aldate's, known as "Bishop King's House," built.

1631. July 26. First stone of the Garden front and lesser quadrangle of St. John's College laid.

1631. Sept. 15. Chapel of Lincoln College consecrated.

1634. West side of University College built.

1635. West side of St. Edmund Hall built.

1635. June 19. Front of University College commenced.

1637. Oriel College quadrangle and hall built.

1639. Chapel of University commenced; finished in 1665.

1639-40. St. Mary Hall Chapel and Hall built.

1640. Staircase of Christ Church Hall built.

1640. Hall of University College commenced; finished in 1657.

1642. June or July. Oriel College Chapel consecrated.

1656. June 26. Chapel of Brasenose College, first stone laid; finished in 1666.

1663. Library of Brasenose College opened.

1665. March 30. Chapel of University College consecrated.

1666. Nov. 17. Chapel of Brasenose College consecrated.

1669. Library of University College opened.

Lector House believes that a society develops through a two-fold approach of continuous learning and adaptation, which is derived from the study of classic literary works spread across the historic timeline of literature records. Therefore, we aim at reviving, repairing and redeveloping all those inaccessible or damaged but historically as well as culturally important literature across subjects so that the future generations may have an opportunity to study and learn from past works to embark upon a journey of creating a better future.

This book is a result of an effort made by Lector House towards making a contribution to the preservation and repair of original ancient works which might hold historical significance to the approach of continuous learning across subjects.

HAPPY READING & LEARNING!

LECTOR HOUSE LLP
E-MAIL: lectorpublishing@gmail.com